Bobby Darin

Bobby Darin

THE INCREDIBLE STORY OF AN AMAZING LIFE

By Al DiOrio

RUNNING PRESS
PHILADELPHIA · LONDON

Contents

A very rare family snapshot—a day in the park for young
Walden Cassotto, right, and family friend Paula Duszik, circa 1939.

Photograph Credits

Cover photograph: Bobby Darin rehearsing at the Gaumont Theatre, London, 1960, © Hulton-Deutsch Collection / CORBIS

Cover photograph inset: © CORBIS

AP / Wide World Photos: pp. 78, 103, 147, 165

© Bettmann / CORBIS: p. 124

© Jim Britt: p. 193

Collection of Vanina Cassotto: pp. 6, 18, 27, 31, 33, 58, 64–65, 86, 98, 118, 128, 133, 148, 150–153, 159, 190, 195

Collection of Al DiOrio: pp. 59, 106, 130

© Allan Grant / Time Life Pictures / Getty Images: p. 74

© Michael Mauney / Time Life Pictures / Getty Images: p. 162

Courtesy of Vana Maffia: pp. 24, 37, 60 (top & bottom), 203

Courtesy of Universal Studios Licensing LLLP: p. 145

Courtesy of Gary Walden: pp. 40–41, 47

Courtesy of Vee Walden: pp. 35, 45 (top & bottom)

Courtesy of Harriet Wasser: pp. 50, 52, 56, 61, 73, 85, 94

Acknowledgments

First, I would like to express my deepest gratitude to Bobby Darin's mother, Ms. Vanina Cassotto, her daughters Vee Vee Walden and Vana Maffia, and her son Gary Walden Maffia for opening up their hearts and lives to me in the hope that this book would accurately portray the man they all loved. This book would not have been possible without their cooperation. Nina's devotion to her son and her children's to their brother is obvious and has made the writing of this book an experience I shall never forget and shall always cherish.

Additionally, there are a few others whose contributions to the book earn them special mention. Their cooperation and support has been invaluable to me and I shall always be grateful to them. These include Anita Buonasorte, Lois Carita, Dick and Kari Clark, Dick and Ellen Lord, Bob and Kay Rozario, Jim Walney, Harriet Wasser, and Ken Young. Special thank yous go to my mother and sister who have worked for hours typing, proofreading, and photostating, in addition to running countless errands. Finally, thanks to David Walley for his valuable help in making the manuscript work, to my editor Alida Becker for her unending patience and invariably sound guidance, and to Buzz and Larry Teacher, who helped turn this dream into reality.

Also to be thanked are: The Academy of Motion Picture Arts and Sciences, AFTRA, Bill Aikens, Joanne Alcaldi, Betty Allen, Tommy Amato (of Las Vegas), Tommy Amato (of Los Angeles), The American Federation of Musicians, Peggy Anastos, Barbara Arrow, ATCO Records, Cheryl Baldino, Frank Barone, Rona Barrett, George Beach, Joyce Becker, Richard and Mickey Behrke, Jim Britt, BMI, the Bronx High School of Science, *The Philadelphia Bulletin,* George Burns, Rose

Burton, Camera Five, CBC-TV, Debbie Campione, Capitol Records, Louis F. Cappelli, Ernest Chambers, Mark Ciechon, Daniel Citrone, Rudy Clark, Bob Crewe, Joe Csida, Dresser Dahlstead, Andrea Darin, Joe Delaney, Mr. and Mr. Quitman Dennis, the Desert Inn, Dion DiMucci, Carl DiOrio, Robert DiOrio, The Director's Guild, Ralph Edwards, Ahmet Ertegun, Laurel Newmark Falken, the Federal Bureau of Investigation, Dr. Josh Fields, Irving Fine, Art Fisher, Sue Forenchak, Francine Forest, Fabian Forte, Connie Francis, Don Galloway, Sara Hoffman Giller, Mimi Greenberg, Don Gregory, Joy Hamann, Brenda Hardin, Mariette Hartley, Marie Herman, Bob Hope, Ira Howard, Ron Howard, Hudson Bay Music, Saul Ilson, Marty Ingels, International Creative Management, Shirley Jones, Wayne Jones, Dr. Leonard Kabel, Murray Kaufman, Roger Kelloway, the offices of Senator Edward Kennedy, the John F. Kennedy Memorial Library, Linda Kloss, Stanley Kramer, *The Las Vegas Sun*, Peggy Lee, *Life* magazine, the Lincoln Center Library, John Lollos, Caroly Lynley, Connie McLaughlin, Mary Jane McQuaid, Charles Maffia, Tom Mankiewicz, Bob Marcucci, Sid Mark, Lou Martinaitis, Joanne Mathewson, David Miller, Tom Monahan, the William Morris Office, Motown Records, Bob Newhart, Edward Newmark, Gertrude Newmark, the New York Foundling Hospital, Donald O'Connor, Gloriana Palancia, Arnie Parious, Joyce Peterson, Mary Phillips, Stephanie Powers, The Producers Guild, Karen Regan, Arthur Resnick, Joan Rivers, Shorty Rogers, *Rolling Stone*, Julia Salerno, Steve Sanders, Russell Sanjac, Elizabeth Santi=oianni, John Santoianni, George Scheck, Arthur Schlesinger, Irwin Schuster, the Screen Actors Guild, Neil Sedaka, Melissa Shuwall, Jean Simmons, Marilyn Singer, Bill Sisca, Stella Stevens, Charlotte Stevenson, Peter Stone, Mark Tan, Marilynn Teacher, Margaret Tod, Mr. and Mrs. Walter Trotter, Mary Ann Venditto, Ted Warwick, Gerry Wexler, Wide World Photos, Duncan Williams, Nancy Wilson, Noreen Woods, and Torrie Zito.

—AL DIORIO

Stratford, New Jersey, 1980

For my grandmother, Margaret Breve,
whose smile makes the darkest days bright.

♪

For my mother, Martha DiOrio,
whose love makes everything easier
and nothing seem impossible.

♪

And for my sister, Barbara DiOrio,
whose laughter and joy for living
make living a joy.

IN MEMORIAM

On the eve of publication, after a long and heroic battle with diabetes, Al DiOrio, longtime friend of Running Press, passed away. His dedication to his work inspired us all, and he will be missed.

I Am

MUSIC AND LYRICS BY BOBBY DARIN

I have left the seed of life
From South Hampton to Singapore.
And if tomorrow morning comes
I guess I'll leave some more.
I'm a captain without an ocean,
And a lover without emotion,
And a monk free of devotion,
But I am, most of all, I am.

I have worn the country's colors
In a thousand different ways.
I have won the game of life
Upon the table which it plays.
I'm a sun without a setting,
And a tear without regretting,
I'm a mind full of forgetting,
But I am, most of all, I am.

Forgive me while I kiss away
This thought that's in my head.
But it's the only proof I have
That this old man ain't dead.
I'm a robin without its wings,
And a song nobody sings,
To the ivy no one clings,
But I am, most of all, I am.
Yes I am, most of all, I am.

♪

Prologue

Las Vegas

The Desert Inn

February, 1971

By the time Bob Rozario and the orchestra had started the opening vamp for "Mack the Knife," Bobby Darin's audience was primed. Dick Lord, his longtime friend, stood in the wings watching. He was continually amazed by the energy Darin produced on stage. "Mack the Knife," the show stopper, always good for an encore, was the song everyone waited for, the one Bobby was famous for.

Tonight was the last show of a long and very successful engagement. After "Mack the Knife," the excitement continued to build from the soft calypso rock of "Work Song" through the upbeat "Higher and Higher" to the mellow James Taylor song "Fire and Rain," which brought many in the audience to the brink of tears. He was killing them tonight, no doubt about it.

As the final strains of "Splish Splash" were being drowned out by the crowd's roar, Lord hurried back to the dressing room. He knew his friend would be feeling pleased. With the audience's applause and cries for encores filtering into the dressing room, Dick watched as Bobby slowly took off his diamond cufflinks.

"Well, Dick, this was the last time we'll ever perform together," he said, quietly giving his startled friend a fierce hug.

"This is the last night of the engagement, sure, but. . . ." Lord laughed nervously, sensing something was up.

"No," said Bobby distantly, "it's the last time we'll work together." He stared off into space. "I'm going into the hospital tonight for open heart surgery. The doctor said my chances are one out of ten. I called the hospital, and they said the last nine people lived, so I guess this is it." His eyes were tearing.

Lord knew now that this wasn't a joke. Time was finally running out for his friend. When he was a child, the doctors had said Bobby would never live to the age of sixteen. As a teenager, he'd told Lord he didn't expect to live to thirty. Now, at thirty-four, Bobby was saying the end was near. It couldn't be.

Dick Lord watched dumbfounded as Bobby changed into jeans and a jacket, pulling the ever-present sailor's cap over his eyes. As the crowd's roar continued outside, Dick began to cry.

Jim O'Neill, the new road manager, entered, "We're ready," he said, as Bobby signaled Lord to follow him out the back exit into the neon-lit Las Vegas night. In the lot was a blue van, its surface reflecting both the Vegas marquees and the starlit sky. Inside was a bed, a reading light, and an assortment of books. Bobby climbed in the back and got into bed. Then O'Neill suddenly appeared with an enormous ice cream sundae. Looking comfortable and calm, Bobby waved goodbye as the door closed and the van commenced its long journey to Los Angeles.

In a daze, tears still in his eyes, Dick Lord returned to Bobby's dressing room. The banging on the door finally brought him round. He opened the door, surveying the crowd of autograph seekers. "Bobby's gone," was all he could say.

♪

Chapter One

"Once you tell a lie, that lie must become the truth for the rest of your life."
—NINA CASSOTTO MAFFIA TO THE AUTHOR, 1979.

Standing at the altar, the priest watched the young couple walk toward him, acutely aware of the opposites they represented. She looked like an innocent, a petite strawberry blond, not much more than nineteen years old. The big man with curly brown hair accompanying her seemed to be a few years older, and he was definitely no innocent. The priest has heard he was connected with the local underworld. No, he would not sanction this union if it was within his power.

He asked the girl, whose name was Polly, to step into his office so that they could talk confidentially. "Why do you want to marry a bum like that?" he bluntly asked her.

"Father, I love him and he loves me," she replied, unshaken.

"But he's wrong for you. He's not your kind," the priest countered.

The girl listened respectfully to his importuning, but in the end she could only repeat her earlier words, "I love him."

Temporarily defeated, the priest called in her beau, Sam, and tried another approach. "Why do you want to marry an American girl? Why don't you marry one of your own?"

Sam couldn't believe his ears. The priest was actually trying to talk them out of marrying. Calmly, he turned on his heels and left the priest in his office. Outside, he took Polly's hand. "We're leaving," he told her.

As they walked down the center aisle of the church, Polly and Sam could hear the priest calling after them, "Please, my children. Come back. Let's talk about this."

They kept right on walking.

The priest was right. In many ways the couple were opposites. Saverio "Sam" Cassotto was the son of an Italian immigrant tailor. His father had come to America immediately after Sam was born and then worked ceaselessly at a shop in Italian Harlem until he had raised enough money to bring his wife, his daughter Margaret, and his son Sam to the new country.

Sam's childhood was placid, unmarred by schooling save for one day, his first. After being teased unmercifully by his fellow students for wearing long pants to school, he begged his father to let him stay home. Despite his lack of formal education, Sam had been a precocious and particularly observent youngster. As an adult, his hobby was to speak all dialects of Italian fluently.

Always enterprising and shrewd, Sam Cassotto found many ways to support himself, by various odd jobs, including cabinetmaking. Sometimes, he found himself in occupations whose legality could be debated. In fact, one of his closest friends was a gentleman by the name of Frank Costello, reputed to be the head of New York's Mafia.

Vivian Fern Walden was the daughter of a successful mill owner from Pascoag, Rhode Island, Frank Walden, whose wife, Julia Hanson, was a native of Racine, Wisconsin. Shortly after Vivian was born, possibly in 1894, Julia and Frank separated, with Julia returning to her family in the Midwest. Eventually she settled in Chicago. She married two more times after her parting from Frank Walden, and became the mother of twin daughters.

As a teenager, Vivian Walden had an adventurous spirit—she often talked of bicycling from Chicago to California in search of excitement. She entered college at a very young age, but left soon afterward to marry Ralph Kennedy, a man she barely knew. Just as impulsively, she packed her bags and moved out a few months later. She then found her first job, as a dancer in a musical review. In a short time, she was a featured player in Weber and Fields musicals and her picture was appearing in all the local papers. It was while touring the country in one of these road companies that she met and married Pasquale Cuomo, rumored to be involved in the Chicago syndicate. This union was also short-lived.

Again she returned to the stage, this time as Paula Walden, The Girl With Three Voices, and got herself a job in a Frank Daniels musical. For a while, she and Daniels were considered something of an item. However, early in 1912, on a layover in Chicago, Vivian, now calling herself Polly, met up with Sam Cassotto, who was in town on business for Frank Costello. She and Sam fell in love, and once Sam's work was done they returned to New York to be married.

After their disastrous encounter with the priest at Our Lady of Mount Carmel, Sam and Polly headed for St. Michael's Episcopal Church in Manhattan. They were married there on Friday, March 1, 1912. In attendance as witnesses were another young couple, friends of Sam who gave their names as Regina and Frank Ross. (Mr. Ross, it should be noted, bore a striking resemblance to the aforementioned Mr. Costello.) After the ceremony, Mr. and Mrs. Sam Cassotto set up house at 227 East 117th Street in Italian Harlem.

This area in the period between 1910 and 1925 was an ethnic enclave not unlike other Italian ghettos of the time in Boston, Philadelphia, and Chicago. During the day, the streets were filled with vendors selling fruit and vegetables from their pushcarts. Women nursed infants on stoops, while older children capered between the carts. Summer evenings often found whole families asleep on the fire escapes outside their buildings.

Although Polly loved her husband dearly, she realized in doing so that she would have to learn to accept her new environment unquestioningly. Her family, on the other hand, felt differently. When her sister Irene visited the city, she was so shocked by Sam and Polly's tenement that she had her cabby return to lower Manhattan immediately, without even setting foot on the ghetto streets. She never returned.

Vivian "Polly" Walden and Saverio "Sam" Cassotto shortly after their marriage in 1912.

Life with Sam wasn't as exciting as Polly had hoped, and again she grew restless. Besides living a life that was totally foreign to her upbringing, she was learning, on a day-to-day basis, how to deal with problems she had never even dreamt of. Drug addition, for starters.

In those days, there were no laws against drug use. Morphine, or morphia as it was sometimes called, was a common painkiller that was used in most over-the-counter patent remedies. In 1907, Sam had contracted a serious internal infection, the result of a poorly performed appendectomy. It took the doctors three months to diagnose the source of the infection, and during that time Sam was in excruciating pain. As was the common practice, he was given regular doses of morphine. After three months, he had become addicted and, once he was released from the hospital, he found it easier to obtain the drug at the local pharmacy than to beat the habit. He was, however, able to get by on the minimum maintenance dose, which was so small that it had almost no outward effect. For all intents and purposes, he was no different from any one of millions who now live on a steady diet of Valium, Librium, or Darvon.

Polly also had a habit that was caused by medical ineptitude. When she first met Sam in Chicago, she was having serious dental problems and was in unbearable pain. As often as possible, she would go to a dentist for relief, but when she couldn't she'd use some of Sam's morphine supply. Eventually, she too became mildly hooked. Both Sam and Polly kept their dependency a carefully guarded secret—hidden even from their closest friends.

On November 30, 1917, after five years of marriage, Polly gave birth to a daughter, Vanina Juliette Cassotto—Nina for short, Italian for "dear little one." Since Sam and Polly had stood as witnesses at Frank Costello's marriage, Italian custom dictated that the Costellos would be Nina's godparents. It was an amiable arrangement, since Sam and Frank were partners in a bar at the time. But before the christening could take place, the two men had an argument, and Costello was out as godfather. It would have been a role with which he was more than familiar.

Around this time, Sam's fortunes started to take a turn for the worse. He began gambling and, as with most gambler's families, the Cassottos' finances became erratic, so Sam resorted to various money-making projects. He tried his hand at inventing, and held a patent for something called a "Lung Testing and Exercising Machine," the success of which was negligible. Another scheme involved selling popsicles, which had recently been invented by an acquaintance of Sam's. He and his family helped out making the frozen orange treats and selling them at South Beach, a Staten Island resort where the Cassottos would often rent a home for the summer. Throughout this period, Sam continued to associate with Frank Costello, and with the advent of Prohibition he filled an important role in the Mafia's rumrunning operation between Canada and the Northeastern United States.

No matter what Sam's occupation at any given time, Polly stood behind her man. Once, after Sam had stolen some foreign currency out of a bank window, Polly brazenly returned it to the same bank, the very next day, to exchange the money for American dollars. The bank never caught on. Her bravado and strength of will were impressive, even to the likes of Frank Costello, who shrewdly remarked to Sam, "If I had Polly behind me, I could do anything."

When the Depression hit, the Cassottos were pushed even closer to the brink. Sam resorted to petty crime to make ends meet, and in 1934 he was arrested for participating in a pickpocket scheme. Despite the fact that this was his first offense, on October 14, 1934, he was conficted and sentenced to a short stretch at Sing Sing Prison in Ossining, New York.

He'd smuggled a small stash of morphine into prison in the heel of his shoe, but after a few days his supply ran out and he went into withdrawal. On October 19, Polly was notified that her husband was sick. She and Nina rushed to his side and spent the afternoon and evening with him. Polly was sure Sam would recover, but she was wrong. The next morning, Polly Cassotto received a telegram from Sing Sing. Sam had died during the night. Cause of death: pneumonia, a frequent side effect of withdrawal.

Polly took Sam's death very hard. She lost a great deal of weight, and her heart weakened dramatically. Stunned by what she knew to be the real cause of Sam's death, she even considered kicking morphine, but her doctor recommended against it, fearing that the shock of withdrawal would be too great for her system. By this time, morphine had become a government-regulated drug, but Polly obtained it legally with her doctor's prescription.

Despite her sorrow over the loss of Sam, or perhaps because of it, Polly's spirit remained strong. She wasn't at all ready to stop living. She passed her strength of spirit on to Nina—that and a strong sense of morality. Throughout her childhood, Nina was taught never to lie and never to steal. Though this ethic would seem at variance with Sam's own shadier professional dealings, it was common enough in Mafia-connected households. But even so, it had more to do with Polly's own moral code than with Sam's. There was only one deviation from the rule: if it was absolutely necessary to tell a lie, you must never, never back down on it; you must live the lie from that day forward as if it were the truth. This was one lesson that Nina was to learn exceptionally well.

Like most Italian fathers, Sam had been especially strict with Nina when it came to boys. They were off limits, in all ways. Nina knew that if her father saw her even talking to a boy, there would be hell to pay. But Polly was of a different mind, and after Sam's death she left Nina free to experiment with her first boy/girl relationships.

In the summer of 1935, Nina, then seventeen, was seeing a young Italian boy who was a few years older than herself. Nature coupled with naivete, and she became pregnant. Since she was naturally a big girl, she was able to hide her condition, even from her mother, while she tried to figure a way out of her predicament. Marriage, even with love, was out of the question. It was awkward: he was in college, his future ahead of him, and she wasn't ready for marriage. Instead, she broke off the relationship and never let her boyfriend know what was wrong. After a few months, she told her mother. Once Polly got over her initial shock, she and her daughter started making plans. They decided that they would move and that the baby would be passed off as Polly's to allay neighborhood gossip.

Luckily, Nina was able to hide her condition—especially from the Home Relief doctor who treated both Polly and Nina for the flu. But their luck didn't hold, and while they were ill, a Home Relief inspector paid a surprise visit to their tenement. Both women were in bed, so no one answered his knock. The inspector returned to his office and filed his report: since there was no one to answer the door, both women were obviously working and no longer needed Home Relief. The checks stopped coming.

To support the family, Nina worked part-time for a neighborhood locksmith. On Tuesday, the twelfth of May, 1936, she reported to the shop as usual. Her boss, Mr. Solomon, ignorant of her condition but sensing her discomfort, suggested that she go home. Soon, she and her mother were on the way to Bellevue Hospital.

It was a beautiful, sunny day, so Polly and Nina decided to walk to the bus stop, where they inadvertently ran into the father of Nina's baby. Nina was shocked. She hadn't seen the man in at least five months. In her loose-fitting clothes, she didn't look pregnant, but she was scared—petrified was more like it. Making small talk, she quaked. Did he know? She suppressed a desire to run, and somehow the minutes passed. The bus arrived, and Nina and Polly were safely on their way again. Nina's child had come as close to his father as he would ever get.

By one that afternoon, Nina had gone into labor. Through the waves of pain, she heard the voice of the attending nurse, "Bear down, mother." To Nina, the last word seemed to spit out like a curse. The delivery, which took forty hours, was accomplished without the help of any anthesia. Finally, at 5:28 in the morning on May 14, 1936, Nina gave birth to a healthy baby boy weighing seven pounds, eight ounces. She had been sure the child would be a boy and had already chosen his name, Walden Robert Cassotto.

Nina and her child remained at Bellevue for two weeks. It was part of the grand design, as she would be passing the child off as her brother once she went home. Nina would not be able to nurse the baby, so it was important that the proper nursing formula be found for young Walden Robert. Eventually it was decided that he would be put on a strict diet of Romanian goat's milk, which sold for five dollars a pound at Depression prices.

From Bellevue, Nina and the baby were sent to the New York Foundling Hospital, a home for unwed mothers, where they were installed in a large dormitory. Presided over by Catholic nuns, the home had a very strict routine. One inflexible rule was that everyone attend early morning mass. Nina was still very weak and one morning, while standing in the first row, she fainted during the service. No one came to her aid. Eventually, she came to on her own and sat down as the mass continued.

Nina spent her time at the Foundling Hospital waiting for her mother's regular visits and reading anything she could get her hands on. After a week, she was able to bring her son home to their new apartment, a third floor walk-up on Second Avenue between 125th and 126th Streets. There were three rooms: a small kitchen, a living room, and a bedroom, as well as a private bathroom, all joined by a long hall. Polly had busied herself during Nina's hospital stay with the moving of the household from their old neighborhood, and she had done her best to make their new home bright and cheery. Like her daughter, she was a voracious reader, and every spared corner of the apartment was crammed with books and magazines.

Once at home, Polly immediately took over the role of mother and Nina that of sister, positions which would never weaken. The baby quickly became the sunshine in both Polly and Nina's lives. In the hospital, young Walden had been prone to uttering such profound phrases as "da da." Because of this, the nurses had taken to calling the baby Dodd. The name held on throughout his childhood.

About a year after the birth of Nina's child, in May of 1937, she met Charles Maffia at a dance club. At the time, Maffia was working as a clerk and truck driver at the R & B Hardware Company, earning $18 a week. Charlie developed an overpowering fondness for Polly's cooking, especially her pies. Before either Nina or Polly realized it was happening, he was spending most of his time in the Cassotto apartment. Finally, after two and a half years of this, Charlie moved in with them.

Bobby Cassotto and Charles Maffia on Easter Sunday 1943.

Charlie was a good provider and the family, although far from well off, was comfortable. What he lacked in earning power, he made up for with enthusiasm and love. Sometimes he would buy a loaf of bread, 10 cents worth of bologna, and 10 cents worth of ham and make a hero. Then he, Nina, and young Bobby would jump in the delivery truck and share the sandwich as well as the deliveries. Somehow, Nina was able to save enough money so that the family could spend most summers at South Beach, just as they had during Nina's childhood.

There was also some government help to supplement Charlie's income. During the Depression, those on Home Relief could go to the food warehouses every Saturday to receive surplus food. On at least one occasion, this also provided an unexpected source of entertainment. One Saturday, when Bobby was about three, Nina came home with nine dozen eggs. Later that day, Bobby was playing in the kitchen, and Nina realized that he was unusually quiet. Fearing the child's silence was a mischievous omen, she got up to check on the boy. Bordering on a state between laughter and tears, Nina beheld her darling Bobby on the floor, rolling the eggs, one at a time, at all the empty bottles he could find in the kitchen.

Even if Bobby was her son by proxy, Polly took on the role of mother with love and determination. She tutored the child as soon as he could talk, raising him to be strong of mind and morals and to do for himself. She taught him that the "I" factor was no sin as long as it didn't hurt anyone else. Above all, she taught him always to give his best effort. If he fell down, she never picked him up—but once he picked himself up, she was always there to brush him off and congratulate him on his accomplishment.

From the earliest days, it was obvious that Bobby would go into show business. Nina had grown up to the songs of Al Jolson, and Charlie loved music too. They played records constantly, and Bobby absorbed it all. Al Jolson became his favorite, but he also loved Charlie's big band music. He and Charlie would often stand in front of the phonograph or the radio, each with a baton, conducting. As he grew older, Bobby came to idolize dancer-comedian Donald O'Connor. Bobby decided that he would be a comedian himself, but the family knew better. "No, no, sweetheart," Polly would argue, "singing, singing!"

It wasn't only music that attracted Bobby—the silver screen gripped his emotions too. Whenever possible, Nina and Charlie would take Bobby to the movies. One of these occasions, when Bobby was only six, seems to stand out from all the rest. They had gone to see *The Pride of the Yankees*, starring Gary Cooper as Lou Gehrig. At one point, toward the end of the film, Cooper gave a rather emotional speech, and it was during this speech that Bobby realized Cooper/Gehrig was going to die. Suddenly, his cries rang through the theater, "Oh my God, he's gonna die! Don't let him die! You can't let him die!"

On July 23, 1942, Nina and Charlie were married. The following year, on May 2, Nina gave birth to her second child, a girl, Vivienne Carla Maffia, nicknamed Vee Vee. At the age of seven, Bobby was told he was an uncle.

Soon after this, Nina and Polly decided it was time to enroll Bobby in school. They took him to P.S. 43 on Brown Place in the Bronx. To their horror, the woman in charge of enrollment spoke of putting him in kindergarten. Polly was aghast. She had spent hours tutoring Bobby in everything from English to history, and she knew this boy was no normal seven-year-old. My God, this boy was intelligent! He knew his numbers, he could read! When the woman snorted in disbelief, Polly dared her to test him. The closest book at hand was thrust at the child, and Bobby proceeded to read from Shakespeare. Polly beamed proudly as the woman agreed this child belonged in first grade. By the end of the term the child advanced to third grade.

Bobby enjoyed school, but it was theatrics that caught his eye, especially if there was a class play. The following year, he was even chosen to be Santa Claus in the Christmas pageant. But on the morning of the performance he woke up complaining of pains in his joints. His temperature was high, and any movement made him scream with pain. The doctor was called, and diagnosed a serious case of rheumatic fever.

With each scream, Polly and Nina's hearts ached, but they never stopped believing that Bobby would recover. They gave him round-the-clock care, with Charlie helping out whenever he was needed. Bobby's illness lasted for several weeks, and then his condition slowly began to improve. Nina and Polly convinced themselves that everything would soon be back to normal.

But nothing would ever again be normal in Bobby's life. Dr. Morris Spindell, the family's physician, brought them a tragic prognosis—if Bobby lived to the age of sixteen, it would be surprising; twenty-one would be too much to ask. The only hope was that somehow medical research might advance to the point where Bobby could be helped. If this

Between the ages of eight and twelve, Bobby suffered four serious attacks of rheumatic fever. This photo was taken at age ten.

were so, and if by some miracle Bobby could hold on until he was in his mid-twenties, there was a faint chance that he could live a normal life. Otherwise, there was no hope that he would ever live past the age of thirty-five.

Between his eighth and twelfth birthdays, Bobby would have four more attacks of rheumatic fever. No attempt would be made to hide the facts—Bobby had to learn to accept the inevitable. From this time on, he took sulfa drugs every day of his life and lived with the knowledge that death could be just around the corner. Years later, he'd still remember the seemingly endless days spent in bed, afraid to move even slightly because of the instantaneous pain. While convalescing, he spent hours reading and working in his coloring books.

Meanwhile, Bobby learned Polly's lessons of truth and honesty well, and took great comfort in her love for him. Just as Nina had earlier, Bobby found that with Polly behind him, he could accomplish absolutely anything. During his absences from school, she tutored him constantly, not only in math and history but in common sense and self-preservation.

Patiently, Polly told him, "You've got to realize the vastness of the world. No matter how important you are, you're only one small person in a world where everybody believes he's just as important as you are. You don't owe anyone anything. I'm your mother. I bore you for nine months, I gave you life, and you don't owe me anything. How could you owe anyone else anything?"

Chapter Two

"It's like I'm in a tunnel, and all the way down at the far end of the tunnel there's a small spot of light. I'm heading toward that light. I'll sacrifice anything I must to reach it. I can't let anything get in the way, because when I reach it, that light will be the world."

—BOBBY CASSOTTO TO NINA MAFFIA, 1952.

Although Bobby had been a top student at Clark Junior High School and had no trouble meeting the academic requirements for admittance to Bronx Science, once there he found the experience unsettling. In 1948, few high schools had as solid a reputation for academic excellence as the Bronx High School of Science, but this wasn't the reason for Bobby's difficulties.

Walden Robert Cassotto simply didn't fit in with most of the other kids at Bronx Science, but he never seemed to understand why. For years, he would blame this on his family's poor social standing and poverty-stricken existence; but in fact they weren't as bad off financially as Bobby seemed to recall. For years, Charles Maffia worked two jobs to see to it that the family—which now included not only Bobby and Vee Vee but also a younger sister, Vana—had food in their mouths and clothes on their backs. While their meals might not have included filet mignon and the clothes might not have been top quality, they never starved, and Bobby never had to wear hand-me-downs.

The fact is, Bobby had already developed the chip on his shoulder that he would later become famous for—a chip he was always waiting for someone to knock off. He wanted to be better than anyone else, so much so that he actually did believe his family was poverty-stricken. And although he loved his family, he felt somewhat embarrassed by them. He knew, for example, that his sister had lived with Charlie for two years before marrying him and that his mother, as brilliant as she was, was dependent on painkillers. Although he never criticized either of them for their lifestyle, he knew that it wasn't what he wanted for himself. Deep inside, he wondered why anyone as intelligent and wise as Polly or as smart as Nina couldn't get out of the Bronx.

Bobby's memories of his feelings during this period remained vivid throughout his life. Shortly before his death, he would tell a friend that the single most embarrassing moment of his life had taken place in a lab class at Bronx Science when a cockroach crawled out of his jacket sleeve as his classmates looked on. It was at Bronx Science that Bobby made up his mind that he would do anything he had to do to get out, to rise above the life he had been born to. He would never be anybody's fool, ever again.

Throughout his childhood, Polly had tried to prepare him for the success she knew would be his. Over and over again, she told him that he was special and that there was nothing he couldn't do. By the time he was at Bronx Science, his determination had reached a fever pitch matched only by hers. The two spent hours huddled together, talking and plotting endlessly until Bobby had come up with a master plan that he would use to map out his every move for the rest of his life.

Bobby told Nina of his plan when he was not more than sixteen. They were on a ferry, returning from South Beach, when he turned to her and spoke for the first time of his desire to make a new life for himself. "Nina, I have a goal in life. It's like I'm in a tunnel and all the way down

Vana and Vee Vee Maffia and Bobby Cassotto, Easter 1949.

at the far end of the tunnel there's a small spot of light. I'm heading toward that light. I'll sacrifice anything I must to reach it. I can't let anything get in the way because when I reach it, that light will be the world."

For a few moments, Nina could only stand there and marvel at this man-child she'd created. She kept remembering the boy who, only four years before, lay near death, and the prayers she and her mother had said for his survival. Now she marveled at his determination. He was ready to take on the world and never doubted he would succeed. Hugging him gently, she replied, "You'll make it, sweetheart, you'll see. God wouldn't have made you suffer the way you did if he didn't have great things in store for you." Then, holding his hand tightly in her own, she thought back over the past as he dreamt of the future.

At Bronx Science, Bobby developed a close friendship with another student, Richard Behrke. Behrke was about Bobby's age and held, some say, a close resemblance to him—fair-skinned and brown-haired, with a cherubic face. He also shared Bobby's love for music. They became inseparable. Behrke's family was somewhat better off than Bobby's, and Bobby spent a good deal of time at their home. Embarrassed by his own less comfortable situation, Bobby seldom reciprocated the hospitality.

Bobby and Richard allied themselves with three more boys at Bronx Science, all of whom shared their love of music: Eddie Ocasio, Walter Raim, and Steve Karmen. During their junior year, the boys decided to form a band. Although Bobby had taught himself to play the piano in the school gym, Ocasio was a better pianist, so he took over that job, with Behrke on trumpet, Walter Raim on guitar, Steve Karmen as vocalist, and Bobby on drums. Bobby had never played the drums before, so he borrowed a set from Dick Lord, an older boy who was a friend of Richard Behrke. The drums were set up in the basement of Bobby's apartment building, and there Bobby practiced every day for three solid months, much to the dismay of the other tenants.

Night after night, the boys would rehearse together, playing fox trots, cha-chas, and big band material from the forties. Each number would be

Walden Cassotto practices his drums during his summer at Sunnylands in 1951.

repeated over and over again, and sometimes the atmosphere became strained as they tried to perfect their amateur skills. Often, however, just when things were getting a little too tense, Bobby would break into a sudden impression of Jerry Lewis or Donald O'Connor, or improvise a crazy lyric like, "Her face was blue, her eyes were red. I spoke to her, but she was dead." The boys would crack up, their mood would lift, and then they'd begin their rehearsal efforts anew.

Soon the boys were ready to work. Their first job was at a high school dance at Bronx Science. They played all night, and when the evening was over the teacher in charge gave them everything he had in his pockets—twenty cents and a stick of gum each. If the band was to amount to anything, they'd need better-paying work.

Gertrude Newmark was day-camp director at a hotel, the Sunnylands, located in the Catskill resort town of Parksville, New York, and if you were a kid she could get you a job. She had started by finding part-time or summer jobs for her own children, Laurel and Eddie, but soon the word spread. Need a job? Ask Mrs. Newmark. Somehow, Steve Karmen heard about her, and soon he and the band were at her doorstep.

The boys learned some of the Jewish songs that were popular in the Catskills and then auditioned in the Newmark living room for Mr. and Mrs. Coccus, the owners of the Sunnylands. They were hired on the spot. The boys would spend the summer of 1951, between their junior and senior years, working for $35 a week. For that princely sum, they would bus tables at breakfast, lunch, and dinner, manage the concessions, and entertain in the evenings.

The Sunnylands was small compared to other Catskill resorts such as Griossinger's and the Concord. At one time, it had been a very large private home which, with a few additions and alterations, had been enlarged to accommodate about a hundred guests. The atmosphere was very cozy, and the food, served family style, was delicious.

It was a busy summer. Bobby had had some trouble with a course that year in school and had to make it up. He would rise at five in the morning and hitch a ride on the milk truck into Liberty, New York, where he would attend summer school in the morning. Then he would get a ride back to the Sunnylands, where he and the boys would start their chores.

This summer not only marked Bobby's first professional engagement, but the first turning of his head to matters of the heart. Mrs. Newmark's daughter Laurel was a pretty girl, and she and Bobby were attracted to each other. Soon the two were going steady and spending most of their time together. They'd write comedy skits which they would perform at

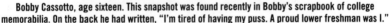

Bobby Cassotto, age sixteen. This snapshot was found recently in Bobby's scrapbook of college memorabilia. On the back he had written, "I'm tired of having my puss. A proud lower freshman was I."

the Sunnylands as well as at some of the other hotels in the area. Usually, these routines would call for Bobby to sing, and it was at one of these performances that Bobby decided he preferred music to comedy.

They were doing a one-night stand at a really big spot on the Catskill circuit, Kline's Hillside Hotel. In addition to their usual comedy skits, Bobby did a song and dance routine reminiscent of Donald O'Connor. That night, for some reason, everything just clicked, and the audience's reaction was fantastic. It was Bobby's first experience with the most addictive drug of all, applause, and he was hooked. It was then that he began to think seriously of a singing career and started testing out various stage names: first Walden Roberts, then Robert Walden.

By the time the summer had ended, Bobby's goal was firmly in place.

He had made up his mind not only to be a singer but to be an all-around entertainer—and, if *he* had anything to do with it, the best entertainer in the business. He wanted to be a legend, and he wanted to do it by the time he was twenty-five. After all, he knew the timetable well—it had been set when he was eight years old.

In June, 1952, at the age of sixteen, Bobby graduated from Bronx Science. That summer, he and the band went back to the Sunnylands for a return engagement, spending their days much as they had a year before and again sharing a cabin with the Newmarks. Bobby and Laurel hadn't seen much of each other since the previous summer, but their relationship picked up where it had left off. It was during this summer that Bobby asked her mother, "Mrs. Newmark, if I was Jewish, would you let me marry Laurel?" Mrs. Newmark just smiled, knowing that they were young and would probably go in different directions soon. She was right. The end of the season also brought an end to the love that had touched Laurel and Bobby those summers at the Sunnylands.

That fall, Bobby enrolled as a theater arts major at Hunter College in the Bronx. After auditioning for several plays and being rejected out of hand, he finally succeeded in winning the second lead in a production of Ibsen's *Hedda Gabler*. He now had his first notice from the campus paper: "Walden Roberts played George Tesman, Hedda's pedantic husband. His performance was imaginative, humorous and perceptive. He succeeded in creating a human being on stage."

Over the next few months, Bobby appeared in many presentations given by the Campus Theater at Hunter. In addition to his role in *Hedda Gabler*, he appeared as the warden in *The Valiant* and had the lead as Judge Samuel Savage in *The Curious Savage*.

Soon after Bobby entered Hunter, he and Richard Behrke rented an apartment at 217 West 71st Street. It was a glorious occasion, their first taste of independence—out of the Bronx and on their own. Their first night there, they made themselves a spaghetti dinner and fought over who should do the dishes. Both were stubborn, and the dishes were placed in the sink, soon to be joined by the next day's breakfast dishes. More dishes were added on successive days. Shortly thereafter, Behrke ran into their old friend Dick Lord at a dance where Lord was playing and invited him over to the apartment. There were dishes in the sink and on the counter, dishes piled at weird, precarious angles everywhere in the small kitchen. Bobby noticed that Lord was staring at the mess. He smiled. "We don't ever have to leave. We live here, we cook here, we do everything here," he announced proudly. Lord mentally added, "Yeah, everything but the dishes," and just laughed, enjoying the happiness of his friends' newfound freedom.

Within a few days, it was obvious that it was time to do something about the dishes. As the three friends entered the apartment, the idea flashed simultaneously in their heads. Silently, they walked into the

For years, the Cassotto and Maffia families spent summers at South Beach, a resort on Staten Island. This shot of Bobby was taken there in the summer of 1953.

kitchen. As Lord held a pillowcase open, Behrke filled it with dishes. When the case was full, Bobby took it over to the window and dropped it onto the trash heap on the sidewalk. Without even mentioning this Keystone Cops slapstick solution to the dish problem, they began to talk about the show they'd seen that night, never missing a beat. That was a special kind of teamwork.

It was easy to toss dishes out a window on a lark, but then what were they going to eat off of? Better, how would they pay for what they were going to eat, even without the dishes? Behrke and Bobby were always broke, but they were cagey. At five in the morning they'd arise to steal bagels from the delivery trucks stopping at the Upper West Side delis. They'd then go home and string their loot across the apartment. The food problem obviously was solved, but soon the electricity went and then the telephone, and that wasn't even funny—though Bobby's flair for comedy often helped brighten their rather drab days.

One day, Dick and Ellen Lord and Bobby were in the S. Klein Department Store on Fourteenth and Broadway. Leaving the store, Bobby grabbed Ellen Lord's pink and white umbrella and burst onto sunny Fourteenth Street, twirling, leaping, and singing. The sight was hilarious. Passersby stopped in their tracks as Bobby, impishly peeking out from underneath the umbrella, pranced down the street. Reaching the corner, he turned, curtsied, closed the umbrella, and entered an occupied taxi. Climbing over the passengers, he exited out the other door and was chased by an irate driver.

Traffic was snarled everywhere as he opened the umbrella again and jumped on the hood of another car. Spellbound, people everywhere stood still and watched. Jumping off the car, Bobby twirled the umbrella over his shoulder and climbed into a truck's cab and dropped the umbrella in the street. As the light changed, the truck crossed Fourteenth Street. The Lords didn't see Bobby again for three days. So much for fun and games.

Bobby was used to being broke, so it never got to him. Fully confident that someday soon he would break through the barrier, he stuck to his master plan and managed to raise fifty dollars to have his first publicity portraits taken. While continuing his education at Hunter, Bobby began spending all of his free time haunting the seemingly endless number of agents' offices up and down Broadway. His publicity photos had been taken to show him as a number of different character types: there were punk shots emulating Marlon Brando, academic poses in which he wore glasses and smoked a pipe, and humorous shots showing him as a sort of Huntz Hall. Naturally, there were also a variety of formal shots done in serious, smiling, and romantic studies.

On the back of each of these photos Bobby had attached fact sheets. Listing his name as Walden Roberts, his height as 5'9", and his weight at 140 pounds, he also went on to claim an incredible number of theatrical credits. These included appearances in such plays as *You Can't Take It With You, Boy Meets Girl, The Children's Hour, Golden Boy, Kiss Me Dudley, The Broad Way,* and something called *X-10 Peraneous.* Also listed were television appearances on the *Kraft TV Playhouse, Take It From Me,* and *The Donald O'Connor Show.* Whether these last few were entirely legitimate credits was a moot point—the energy that motivated Bobby to these small excesses was what mattered.

This, of course, was 1953, just prior to the McCarthy hearings. Hundreds of people in the entertainment industry were being blacklisted for alleged communist activities, and Walden Roberts did not intend to find himself on that list. The last entry on his fact sheets read as follows: "I rattle off lines in the following dialects: British, French, Italian, Spanish, German, Irish, Jewish, Swedish AND Russian. (The capitalization of the word "and" in no way reflects my political beliefs, it merely was a slip on the machine.)"

Bobby's canvassing of agents' offices eventually paid off. The Salome Gaynor Theater for Children needed a bad Italian for their production of *Kit Carson.* It was the break he needed. Bobby dropped out of Hunter in December of 1953 to join the seven-week tour at a salary of $45 a week.

It was on this tour that Bobby met a thirty-one-year-old Spanish dancer who was about to embark on a tour of the Northeast. She asked Bobby to join her act and play the bongos. But bongos turned out to be

the furthest thing from her mind—and his. It was the beginning of a tempestuous love affair. Their relationship was stormy from the first, and on at least two occasions Bobby had to save her after suicide attempts. Early on, she had him help her perform an abortion on herself using a wire clothes hanger.

The affair was not only emotionally draining, it was standing in the way of the Cassotto master plan. Bobby did everything he could to cut loose, but he was helpless. Whenever he tried to leave, his lover would threaten suicide. Finally, after six months, they reached the breaking point. One night they began arguing. She told him scornfully that he would never amount to anything in show business—then she packed her bags and left him.

For months, Bobby was numb. All of Polly's old warnings had been borne out with a vengeance. Bobby realized then that the world wasn't going to look out for him, that he had to take care of himself. He'd have to discipline himself. Each move would have to be thought out carefully. If not, if he acted without discretion, he might very well remain right where he was for the rest of his life, no better than the thousands of others with show business aspirations who were still pounding the pavements of New York.

Even after their split, and for years later, the memory of this relation-

In 1953, Bobby saved up enough money to have his first publicity pictures taken. They included a variety of formal portraits as well as character studies such as these showing Bobby posing as Marlon Brando, Huntz Hall, and Mr. Peepers.

ship lingered on. In January 1959, five years after their separation, Bobby's former lover took a fatal overdose of sleeping pills. She was found in a Toronto hotel room, dressed in a nun's habit. Her hands were clasped over a crucifix, and she was surrounded by burning candles. Bobby finally took stock of their time together: "Before I met her, I was just like any other kid in the Bronx. Afterward, I was the most disillusioned human being in the world. But I was no kid!"

After this affair had ended, Bobby moved back to the apartment on 71st Street and tried to pick up his career where he had left off. College was out—and music, not acting, consumed Bobby and Behrke's time. They spent most nights at the Club 78, a small neighborhood spot at 78th and Broadway. It was "the" hangout uptown where all the unemployed musicians gathered to bitch and jam to their hearts' content. It was here that Bobby developed a solid respect for jazz, where he learned the rich lore of the business. He sat spellbound at the feet of the old-timers as they reminisced about the Big Band Era and what it was like to work for greats like Billie Holiday, Peggy Lee, Judy Garland, Frank Sinatra, Nat King Cole, and Bing Crosby. Their stories fired his imagination and hardened his resolve to do anything he could to work with these legends himself.

Around this time, Bobby began putting his lyric-writing talents to work by collaborating with another Bronx Science graduate, Don Kirshner, who was writing radio spots for local businesses. One of their earliest and most successful efforts was a plug for a local furniture store:

135 Springfield Avenue,
Seven big showrooms
Roger builds for you.
If you're buying furniture
Stop in today.

You had to be there. . . .

Somewhat less successful was the jingle Bobby and Donny wrote for a small German airline. The lyric was catchy, but the music was all wrong. For background they used the opening bars of Beethoven's Fifth, then associated with the Nazi movement. Scratch one artsy commercial.

Obviously, writing jingles for German airlines was a dead-end pursuit. It wasn't the kind of airplay the boys were looking for. No, they had to go for the outside lucky shot that would get Bobby's career into high gear. On a hunch, they went to see George Scheck, a former vaudevillian and choreographer who managed a number of rising entertainers, including—fatefully enough for Bobby—young Connie Francis.

Scheck was also the host of a weekly television variety program called *Star Time.* When Bobby and Donny brought Scheck their first tunes, he was so impressed that he asked them to write the theme song for his show. Shortly thereafter, Scheck placed a few of their songs. LaVern Baker sang "Love Me Right," Bobby Short did "Delia," Davy Hill recorded "By My Side," and the Jaye Sisters took both "Real Love" and "School's Out." None of the songs were hits, but the boys were on their way.

For Bobby, songwriting was less important than a singing career, and this was putting a strain on his partnership with Kirshner, who was also acting as Bobby's manager. It seemed inevitable that they would come to a parting of ways. Finally, one night when Dick and Ellen Lord,

Kirshner, and Bobby were having dinner together in a restaurant, Bobby laid it all on the line. "Donny," he said sadly, "I really love you and I respect you, but nothing's happening. If nothing happens within the next few months, then I can't let you be my manager anymore." Kirshner's eyes welled up with tears.

The writing partnership continued a bit longer, despite Bobby's growing ambition. There were a few more successful radio spots, and whatever dates Bobby could get Donny took care of, but they were strictly obscure. Their songwriting also continued to limp along.

One day, Donny and Bobby walked into Scheck's office with a song called "My Teenage Love." Scheck looked it over, thought it was worth a shot, and told the boys to take it upstairs to the recording studio and have a demo made using the in-house girls. A few hours later they returned, and as Scheck set the tape up for playback, Bobby began to talk. Scheck shushed him and settled back in his chair. But he wasn't hearing a girl singing.

"Who is that?" Scheck demanded.

No one answered. Bobby just looked sheepish; he'd never discussed his singing ambitions with Scheck.

The revelation hit Scheck hard. He was flabbergasted. "You mean you sing too?"

Bobby nodded.

George Scheck leaned back in his chair and smiled. "Start thinking of a professional name," he said, "because in a week you're going to need one for your recording contract."

♪

Chapter Three

"You'll vomit when you hear it."

—BOBBY DARIN TO RICHARD BEHRKE AFTER RECORDING
"SPLISH SPLASH," APRIL 1958.

"What's in a name," Bobby mused. A few months before his meeting with George Scheck, Bobby and Nina had driven past a Chinese restaurant whose sign was flashing. The neon letters M-A-N were burned out of the name MANDARIN so that the name read DARIN. "Hmm, Darin. . . ." Bobby remarked. "Darin, that would be a great stage name. Bobby Darin."

Walden Robert Cassotto changed his name to Bobby Darin in a few hours; it took George Scheck just three days to sign him with Decca Records—and to become his personal manager as well. Now the ball was rolling. Scheck went to Milt Gabler, an executive at Decca who was so knocked out by Bobby's demo that he immediately put him to work recording "Rock Island Line," a song that had been a minor success earlier that year for a British skiffle singer, Lonnie Donegan.

The year 1956 also marked the debut of another legend. In January, RCA released "Heartbreak Hotel" by Elvis Presley. In March, Presley made his network debut on *Stage Show,* a weekly television series produced by Jackie Gleason and hosted by the Dorsey Brothers. Presley was such a smash that he was immediately asked to return two weeks later. It

(top and bottom) In the spring of 1956, Bobby appeared at dozens of small clubs throughout the East and the Midwest. These two shots were taken during one of the performances on this tour.

was between the Presley appearances that Scheck, with the help of Decca, booked Bobby Darin for his television debut, four days after he'd signed with the label and just two since he'd recorded "Rock Island Line."

The night before the show, Bobby was rehearsing at George Scheck's office when Donny appeared, quite distraught. Bobby, it seemed, had collected twenty-one outstanding traffic tickets for parking violations. The police not only had a summons out but had discovered that he would be at the Dorseys' studio the next day and were intending to arrest him before he could go on. While Bobby sat and stewed quietly in embarrassment, George Scheck rushed out and paid the four hundred dollars in fines. There'd be time enough later on to repay the favor, he told Bobby.

The opening night jitters hit Bobby hard, despite Scheck's four-day prep. In fact, Bobby was so scared he'd forget the lyrics to "Rock Island Line" that he wrote them on the palm of his hand. Bobby was fine when the cold red eye of the camera came on, but when he made a broad theatrical gesture with his hands he noticed that his palms were sweating profusely. The lyrics were one sweaty mess, and for a moment he lost his composure and timing. Then he started to shake all over.

No, the public didn't take notice of Bobby Darin on that March evening. Presley had made too strong an impact, and Bobby's shaky performance, coupled with his lackluster material, just didn't make it. It was an inauspicious public debut, but it was a start nonetheless. Immediately after the Dorsey show, Bobby headed for Detroit, where he had been signed for his first nightclub performance. Steve Karmen, his old high school buddy, went along to accompany him on the guitar.

A few days later, George Scheck got a frantic telephone call from the club manager. He thought he'd booked a single act and here were Darin and Karmen working as a team! Immediately, Scheck flew to Detroit. It was true. Bobby had had such a case of stage fright that he'd asked Karmen to be his prop and work duets. Needless to say, Scheck left with Karmen in tow. A few days later, Bobby had recovered his composure,

Bobby's appearance on the Dorsey Brothers' television show went almost totally unnoticed, as did most of his Decca releases. Nevertheless, ads of the day conveniently ignored these facts.

and after the gig in Detroit he went on to tour several small clubs in the Midwest and Northeast. Self-assurance grew with each new engagement.

Back in New York, Bobby quickly recorded four more singles in a bewildering variety of styles. His second release, "Silly Willy," was a Darin-Kirshner composition that represented fifties rock at its most banal. "Hear Them Bells," backed by "The Greatest Builder," was a semireligious, inspirational tune. "Dealer in Dreams," another obscure release, followed. The well-known Darin style and voice were still a long way off.

During the following year, Bobby spent more time touring the East and Midwest, appearing in a string of small clubs: the Cabin Club in Cleveland, the Purple Onion in Indianapolis, Mike's South Pacific in Birmingham, and the Safari in New Orleans. He was billed as "Bobby Darin, Star of the Dorsey Brothers TV Show."

His recordings may have been undistinguished, but Bobby was catching fire on stage—sometimes too much. One week, he opened at the Safari Club in Long Island for Della Reese. The first show was a smash, except for the star. Della was incensed at being upstaged by this brash upstart. She complained to the manager, and during the remaining of the engagement she opened for Bobby so she could get first crack at the audience.

Bobby Darin's career may have been on the move, but George Scheck also had other budding stars to keep an eye on—namely another singer named Connie Francis. Constance Franconero had begun taking accordion lessons at the age of four, and by the time she was eleven she was performing professionally. At the age of twelve, she appeared on George Scheck's radio show *Star Time* and entered and won Arthur Godfrey's *Talent Scout* show. Soon after Scheck signed her she was recording for MGM Records.

Just as Bobby was going through his trial by fire at Decca, Connie was suffering through her own at MGM, which coincidentally included the recording of a Darin-Kirshner tune, "My Teenage Love." Throughout 1956 and 1957, Bobby and Connie ran into each other at George Scheck's office and even appeared on the same bill at various rock and roll shows in the New York area. Both managed by George Scheck (part of the same family, as it were), Connie and Bobby soon became very close.

Bobby referred to Connie as his "sweetheart" and told everyone he wanted to marry her. She, he confessed, was the kind of girl he wanted to spend his life with and, more important, she was the kind of girl he wanted to be the mother of his children. Marriage was inevitable, save for one stumbling block—Mr. Franconero, Connie's father, was dead set against his daughter marrying *anyone*. He had worked hard, she was going to be a star, and no bum from the Bronx was going to ruin everything. He warned George Scheck repeatedly that Connie and Bobby were not to see each other, that Scheck was not to be a party to any secret rendezvous. But Connie and Bobby were unconcerned; after all, they were in love. Soon Franconero gave Scheck an ultimatum: break them up or lose Connie as a client.

The next day, Scheck met with Bobby to discuss the situation. Bobby knew Scheck was upset, but he couldn't imagine what was wrong. They'd become very close over the last year. George had done a great deal to groom Bobby for success; he'd even loaned him over fifteen hundred dollars for a wardrobe, musical arrangements, and other expenses.

Scheck spoke quietly and steadily. "You know, I think you have a great career ahead of you," he said calmly. "You're going to be a big star, but Connie was here first. My loyalties must remain with her. You're going to have to find another agent." Bobby sat there staring at his shoes. He understood Scheck's position, but he didn't know what to say. It seemed like a bad dream.

Bobby left the agency, but he and Connie still continued to see each other. Later that year, when Connie was waiting to appear on *The Ed Sullivan Show,* Bobby came over to watch her rehearse. Unbeknownst to him, Connie's father got wind of it. Suddenly, Scheck received a frantic phone call. Connie's father was on the way to the theater with murder on his mind.

Just as Scheck hung up, Franconero was heard storming in. Bobby and Connie looked at each other, terrified, not knowing which way to turn first. George Scheck and Dick Lord ran downstairs and stalled Connie's father while Bobby climbed out a men's room window and ran down the fire escape. So much for that romance.

Though their love affair was thwarted, Connie and Bobby remained close professional friends. Two years later, in 1959, they appeared together on *The Ed Sullivan Show* and sang two duets. "You're the Top," a Cole Porter classic, capped the evening and publically summed

Bobby's romance with Connie Francis fizzled because her father opposed the match. Several years later they were reunited by the Heart Association, serving as King and Queen of Hearts. After being named King of Hearts for three consecutive years, Bobby was asked to hold the position permanently.

up their feelings for each other. Now they both were stars, and irate fathers with guns could harass them no more.

Guns aside, Bobby Darin had enough trouble dealing with his budding career. He'd lost a manager, and now he was about to lose his deal with

Decca. Since he wasn't selling any plastic, they were rapidly losing interest. The material they were giving him didn't help either. Once again he had to take matters into his own hands.

While appearing at Mike's South Pacific in Birmingham, Alabama, Bobby had developed some close ties with the local disc jockeys and musicians, and they loaned him enough money to record a few songs on his own. One of these was the old Billy Rose song, "I Found a Million Dollar Baby (In a Five and Ten Cent Store)." Demo in hand, Bobby approached Ahmet Ertegun of Atlantic Records. Ertegun was impressed.

Atlantic Records had been founded in 1948 by three men: Ahmet Ertegun, his brother Neshui Ertegun, and Herb Abramson. The Erteguns conceived of their company as a home for rhythm and blues artists who were having a hard time finding work at the more traditionally oriented record companies such as Columbia, Capitol, and RCA. The clientele at Atlantic and its subsidiary ATCO then included Joe Turner, Ruth Brown, LaVern Baker, Morgana King, and one of Bobby's idols, Ray Charles.

Atlantic Records was rapidly developing a strong reputation as an up-and-coming place for young performers, especially for rock and roll. Early rock was a blend of rhythm and blues and country music. The latter had always drawn something from the blues. After all, country-oriented singers like Jimmy Rogers, Carl Perkins, and Elvis Presley crossed the line from country into watered-down rhythm and blues, which Alan Freed, the granddaddy of all New York deejays, would christen "rock and roll." Above all, Atlantic was willing to take chances, and that's all Bobby Darin really needed.

In the late spring of 1957, ATCO released Bobby's recording of "Million Dollar Baby." Another solid miss to be sure, but having the contract and the Ertegun energy behind him opened a few doors, one of which led to the legendary Murray Kaufman, a.k.a. Murray the K, one of the top rock and roll disc jockeys in New York. Kaufman took an instant liking to Bobby and began featuring him in his rock shows at Harlem's Apollo Theater.

It was some baptism. The rest of the bill included top black rock and roll acts such as Billy Ward and the Dominoes, the Five Satins, and the Chantels. During this era, white performers were taking a big chance working to all-black audiences, especially sandwiched within an all-black revue. The audiences at the Apollo were brutal with white mediocrities. You had to be good or be gone. Bobby was better than good. He rose to the occasion and was great.

Darin's act at the Apollo consisted of a few Fats Domino numbers, "Million Dollar Baby," and his own impersonations of Ray Charles. This latter bit could have been especially disastrous, but the audiences greeted each of Bobby's performances with enthusiastic applause. Critics were cool to him, though. One review, in *Variety,* commented that

After five unsuccessful releases, Bobby left Decca Records and signed with ATCO. Publicity shots taken around this time show the polished Darin image emerging.

"Darin is a young rock 'n' roller who has to learn that it takes more than a blaring voice to be a winner. His style is overpowering, and he needs experience in delivery."

Bobby took the critic's advice and went back on the road. Over the next few months, he set out to polish his act through another extensive tour of small clubs. His salary during this period ran the gamut from $175 a week at Ken Wa Lou's in Toledo, Ohio, to $300 a week at Mike's South Pacific in Birmingham, and $200 for two days at the Erie Social Club in Philadelphia.

He didn't neglect his recorded output either. Between the release of "Million Dollar Baby" in the spring of 1957 and May of 1958, Bobby Darin recorded and released two more singles on the ATCO label, "Don't Call My Name" and "Just in Case You Change Your Mind." But the tunes stiffed on the charts, and again his contract was up for renewal. Bobby was becoming frustrated. Rock and roll was far from his favorite musical idiom. Besides, he had intended to use whatever success he had as a rocker as a stepping stone to other areas of show business. At this rate, he'd never make it.

Pressure continued to mount. He knew that unless he came up with something hot, ATCO would drop him. In order to have a record ready for release when his ATCO contract expired, he recorded two songs on the Brunswick label, "Early in the Morning" and "Now We're One." Brunswick prepared to release the record under the group name, "The Ding Dongs." Possibly he'd covered himself.

Other forces were working behind the scenes. Even in the music business, friendship counted for something. Bobby had continued to keep in touch with Murray Kaufman after the Apollo gigs, and the two had become close. Bobby was still without a manager or an agent, so Kaufman did whatever he could to line up jobs. Through Kaufman, Bobby got a featured spot on the Dean Martin *City of Hope Telethon* and also on a Martha Raye special.

When Bobby was in New York, he spent a great deal of time at Kaufman's apartment. There he'd pound away at the piano, write music, or just spin out tales of what he hoped would be. Fittingly enough, it was in Kaufman's living room that his dream would be realized.

Murray Kaufman's mother, Jean Murray, was a frustrated songwriter and often would suggest song titles to her son. One day, while Bobby and Murray were sitting in the Kaufman apartment, Kaufman's mother called in with another one of her outrageous suggestions. This time her title was "Splish Splash, Take a Bath." Kaufman told Bobby the title over a cupped phone. They both groaned. Then Bobby said, rather casually, "You know, I could write a song with that title." Kaufman laughed, and then retired for a shower and a change of clothes. When he returned to the living room, less than an hour later, Darin had finished composing "Splish Splash."

Things looked black at ATCO when Bobby brought around "Splish Splash." Herb Abramson, who'd produced Bobby's other three releases, passed on it entirely. Jerry Wexler, another ATCO staff producer, heard the tune but thought it was garbage. Luckily, Ahmet Ertegun was of a different mind. He knew that if Bobby didn't have a hit record, business economics made it inevitable that he'd be dropped from the label. He didn't want to let Bobby go without one good shot, so he decided to produce this single himself. If it didn't work, Bobby would be let go.

"Splish Splash" was recorded without overdubbing. To make it work out economically, Ertegun recorded two sides with Morgana King. Four sides were recorded in three hours—something had to hit out of that session, he hoped.

Bobby, on the other hand, had no illusions about this new tune. He knew it wasn't a great piece of music, and the lyrics were far from being deathless prose, but maybe the kids would dig it. If not, he was out on the streets again. There were many misgivings. He even told Behrke, "You'll vomit when you hear it. I've gone all the way with the bastardized sound, but I'm blowing a bundle on this one."

Chapter Four

"I have a rock and roll hit. That makes me one of a thousand other guys. I have to go beyond rock and roll. I have to prove I can sing."

—Bobby Darin, 1958.

There was only a slight chill in the air when Bobby left the ATCO studios on that fateful evening of April 10, 1958, after recording "Splish Splash." It was late and there weren't many taxis around, so he walked the few short blocks to Hanson's Drug Store, where his closest friends were waiting to help him celebrate.

Hanson's Drug Store was a typical neighborhood drugstore in a neighborhood that was hardly typical. Located on the corner of Fiftieth Street and Seventh Avenue, Hanson's was a block away from the theater where Ed Sullivan's weekly variety show was telecast; a couple of blocks east of the ABC, CBS, and NBC television studios; and right down the street from the Brill Building, headquarters for hundreds of songwriters and agents. Inside, Hanson's looked like a hundred other drugstores in New York City. Rows of package goods, a prescription counter and, of course, a soda fountain. There were booths in the back, counter service, and a juke box. It was a convenient spot for Bobby and his friends to meet, a music business mecca. It also played a central role in Bobby's creative life.

Sliding into the aluminum and leatherette booth, he smiled and said hello to Steve Karmen, Don Kirshner, Richard Behrke, Dick and Ellen Lord, Harriet Wasser, and a few others. The atmosphere was warm, friendly, and supportive. All his friends were aware of the pressure he was feeling. It was now or never. Harriet had a camera with her and asked Bobby to stand by the juke box so that she could immortalize the occasion on film. Then, after coffee and some more talk, the group broke up and everyone went home. It was just a matter of waiting now.

A year before, Bobby had met Harriet Wasser at Hanson's. She was having coffee at the counter when Bobby sat down next to her. At the time, she was working as a PR rep and secretary for Steve Lawrence and Eydie Gorme. She knew who Bobby was and struck up a conversation. By the

After recording "Splish Splash," Bobby stopped at Hanson's Drug Store. Spirits were high, and Bobby was asked to pose by the juke box to commemorate what was sure to be a special night.

time the coffee was done, she had agreed to do Bobby's PR for no salary. She just knew he'd make it.

Once the irrepressible energy of Harriet Wasser had been combined with the irrepressible talents of Bobby Darin, a special chemistry had been formed. Harriet was nothing if not persistent. If she thought someone could help Bobby's career, she would corner them anywhere—in coffee shops, supermarkets, record stores; on street corners, at radio stations, and on the telephone. She plagued them, she cajoled them. They had to listen to Bobby, they had to put an item in their column or play his record. Basically, they had to do *something*. And, little by little, they did.

Shortly after the recording of "Splish Splash," Bobby was asked to appear at a record hop being hosted by Dick Clark at the Berwyn Skating Rink on Philadelphia's Main Line. Clark himself was quite a success story. He had started his broadcasting career at WRUN in Rome, New York, in 1949. By 1955, he was the host of his own afternoon television show, *Bandstand,* a local Philadelphia dance program. In August 1957, the show was picked up by the national ABC network and televised as *American Bandstand.* All this while Clark was still in his mid-twenties!

Dick Clark had a knack for discovering, merchandising, and popularizing such teen idols as Paul Anka, Frankie Avalon, Dion, Jimmy Darren, and Bobby Rydell. In addition to playing their records, he'd often have them guest on his show, as well as take them to various local record hops. Like the legendary Alan Freed, he also organized marathon rock shows and toured them throughout the country. Clark was the only man who could guarantee Bobby national exposure with the right audience. It was crucial that things go well.

When he arrived at Clark's Bandstand offices prior to the hop, Bobby was in a particularly jovial frame of mind. Motioning Clark to be seated, Bobby put his single on the turntable, and the sound of "Splish Splash" filled the room. Bobby moved in time to the music, a pantomime performance. "Well, Sir Richard, what do you think?" Bobby asked nervously.

Bobby and his public relations rep, Harriet Wasser, circa 1958.

"Robert, I think you've finally done it!" said Clark.

Bobby breathed a sigh of relief. "I think so, too!" he added, almost laughing with joy.

When Bobby and Dick arrived at the Berwyn Skating Rink, both made their way to the makeshift plywood stage. Dick started his show, worked the crowd, and played some tunes. For the most part, Bobby was ignored, save for the occasional bobby-soxer who recognized him and wanted an autograph.

Then Clark announced, "We have a special guest star this evening. He's got a new record that's very exciting. Let's give him a big hand and welcome Bobby Darin!" There was only scattered applause.

Lip-synching to the record, Bobby mugged and danced as if he was opening at the Copa. By the time he finished, the audience was his. After taking his bows, Bobby ran into the makeshift bathroom/dressing room.

"When can I have a copy of the record for the show?" Dick asked as Bobby finished toweling off his sweat-drenched hair. Bobby explained that it wouldn't be released for two weeks, but that he could have a copy to Dick the following Monday.

"Good," Clark replied, "Now one more thing. Can you do the song on the show in two weeks?"

"I think maybe I can fit it in," Bobby grinned, "but first I'll have to speak to my social secretary."

Dick Clark had spotted another winner. The record became an overnight smash, and Bobby Darin was firmly entrenched as a top teen hero. The day the success of "Splish Splash" was assured, Harriet Wasser was put on salary as Bobby's personal assistant.

Soon after "Splish Splash" was released, Ahmet Ertegun took Bobby to visit Csida-Crean Associates, one of the first three-way music conglomerates in the industry. Joe Csida and Charles Crean owned a talent management organization, a record and television production company, and

Darin with some of his closest friends, circa 1958. Left to right: Richard Behrke, Dick Lord, Bobby, Steve Karmen, and Ellen Lord.

two music publishing outlets, Towne Music with ASCAP and Trinity Music with BMI. The men had recently scored a tripleheader when two of their writers, Bob Davie and Marvin Moore, had written a song entitled "Green Door." Csida-Crean produced a recording of the song by one of their own singers, a New York disc jockey named Jim Lowe. It went on to become one of the biggest selling singles of the fifties. Other singers handled by Csida-Crean at the time were Betty Johnston, Eddie Arnold, and Santo and Johnny.

Bobby Darin with some of his contemporaries: Fabian Forte, Duane Eddy, Jimmy Clanton, and Bobby Rydell. These photos were taken during one of Bobby's many rock tours in the late fifties.

Darin strikes a pensive pose backstage at the Brooklyn Paramount Theater.

Although Bobby cockily told friends that he was interviewing agents instead of vice versa, he worked hard to win the admiration of Joe Csida, Charles Crean, and their associate Ed Burton during that initial meeting. In just a few short minutes, he sang two songs, did an imitation of a Chinese waiter, and then, shoving a cigar in his mouth and jumping on top of the piano, did his impression of Groucho Marx. The men were dumbfounded. When Bobby told them he was going to be an enormous success, Burton thought, "This kid is nutty, but he's right." Before leaving the office, Bobby had signed with the agency.

The Csida-Crean agency began putting together a master plan of its own. Although the prime objective was to get Darin into major nightclubs, Joe Csida understood the importance of the teen market to Bobby's career. In October of 1958, they booked Bobby on a seventeen-day rock show tour that included Frankie Avalon, Clyde McPhatter, the Coasters, and Buddy Holly and the Crickets. The tour was an enormous success, and Bobby and Buddy Holly, the stars of the tour, enjoyed working together. So much so, in fact, that Holly invited Bobby to join Richie Valens, Dion and the Belmonts, the Big Bopper, and himself on a tour of the Midwest, set for February of 1959. Bobby appreciated the invitation, but he was overbooked. But for that, he might have been on board on February 2 when Holly's plane crashed, leaving no survivors.

Bobby made his first major nightclub appearance in December 1958 at Ben Maksik's Town and Country in Brooklyn. Months of preparation had gone into this move, and Bobby's performance had all the polish of a nightclub veteran. Included in his program were an even mix of rock hits such as "Splish Splash" and "Queen of the Hop," rhythm numbers such as "Blue Monday" and "Hallelujah, I Love Her So," and standards such as "Where Is the One" and "Some of These Days." *Variety* found Bobby's on-stage manner "ingratiating" and his singing "a lot of fun," also noting that he had "considerable savvy and knows the score musically."

For Darin, everything had changed. In 1957, after expenses, Bobby had earned $1,600. In 1958, with the success of "Splish Splash" and club dates all over the country, his income had skyrocketed to $40,000 after expenses—not a bad jump.

In July of 1958, ATCO released Bobby's first album, entitled *Bobby Darin*. It included some of his earlier, less successful work for ATCO, some new material recorded just for the album and, of course, "Splish Splash." Bobby had written seven of the twelve songs—five with Don Kirshner and one with Woody Harris.

Throughout 1958, Bobby made dozens of local and network television appearances plugging "Splish Splash." "Early in the Morning," released soon after the success of "Splish Splash," was another hit. Then, in October 1958, ATCO released Bobby's recording of "Queen of the Hop," his third major hit in a row. Bobby's string of record successes would continue in January 1959, with the release of his recording of "Plain Jane."

There was no stopping Bobby now—especially once he had teamed

up with a young agent by the name of Steve Blauner. Bobby's relationship with Blauner was to change the direction of his entire career, but
had it not been for a rift between Blauner and the William Morris office,
he and Bobby might never have met.

Steve Blauner was a big guy with thinning hair and a face full of
freckles. Two years older than Bobby, Blauner had made his mind up,
after sitting through *The Jolson Story* thirteen times as a youth, to enter
show business—any way he could. After taking time out for a stint in the
Air Force and classes at New York Univesity, he set about becoming an
artists' representative.

One fateful evening, he walked up to Sammy Davis at the
Copacabana and informed him, "The way you feel about Frank Sinatra
is the way I feel about you." At the time, Davis was under contract to
the William Morris Agency and Blauner was a booking agent for
General Artists Corporation. The two men spent a great deal of time
together, and soon William Morris began accusing Blauner of trying to
steal their client. Blauner was insulted and resolved to get even. During
this flap, William Morris was trying to sign up Bobby Darin. News of
this reached Blauner, who promptly signed Bobby to a personal management contract for GAC.

Soon afterward, Joe Csida and Ed Burton (Bobby's agent at Csida-
Crean) scored a major coup in arranging a British tour for Bobby at a
salary of $1,900 a week. Meanwhile, Blauner, through inspired sales-
manship and some arm-twisting, had comedian George Burns offer
Bobby the opening spot in his first Las Vegas nightclub act. The salary
was smaller, but the prestige was incalculable. "Cancel the British tour,"
Bobby demanded. "We can't, we're committed," Burton countered.
"Then get uncommitted," was Bobby's reply.

The Darin/Burns combination was a smash from the start. Burns was
already a forty-year show biz veteran, a theater and vaudeville legend.
Bobby could have no better mentor. Burns opened the show with a
monologue and then introduced Bobby. After half a dozen songs by
Darin, Burns returned for a song and dance, followed by a closing duet of

Bobby sings "I Ain't Got Nobody" as he and George Burns
do a sand dance during their nightclub act.

"I Ain't Got Nobody." "He was sensational," Burns would later recall.
"After my introduction, Bobby would go out there and kill them!"

Offstage, George Burns and Gracie Allen welcomed Bobby into their
lives as one of the family. Bobby had an enormous amount of respect for
George Burns, and never called him anything but Mr. Burns. On one
occasion, he remarked to the press, "Mr. Burns is a father symbol to me,
and you can omit the word symbol." They spent hours working
together, with the old trouper giving Bobby the benefit of his experience.
Usually the advice was warmly accepted.

One night, the two men were onstage and about to go into their sand
dance. The stage business required that a small amount of sand be sprin-
kled on the floor, and then a soft-shoe dance was done over it. Both
Darin and Burns kept the sand in the pockets of their tuxedos. However,
when the time came to sprinkle the sand, Bobby told Burns he'd forgot-
ten it. Burns made no comment then, but backstage he lectured Bobby

on his sloppiness. He had never spoken crossly to Bobby before, and the young singer's feelings were hurt.

Later on, Burns regretted the way he had yelled and sought Bobby out at a nearby coffee shop. As he walked in, he saw Bobby having an argument with a girl he'd been dating and watched her storm out in a huff.

Burns walked over and gently said, "Gee, Bobby, I'm sorry, but that's life."

Bobby simply looked up and said, "That's all right, Mr. Burns. I've learned my lesson. As a matter of fact, I've got the sand in my pocket right now!"

Other times, though, Burns' advice was ignored. During the engagement, Bobby won $2,500 at the gambling tables. Of course, he bragged about his luck. Burns was pleased, but cautioned him not to go back to the casino and lose the money as easily as he'd won it. George even offered to hold Bobby's winnings until they left Vegas, telling him, "You're too young to lose all of that money, even though you won it."

But Bobby cut him off. "I'm old enough to take care of myself," he

Backstage, George Burns gives Bobby some last minute advice on their opening night in Las Vegas.

snorted. Inevitably, Bobby lost it all. Just before show time, Burns learned what had happened and proceeded to chew out his young protege. In one of his more obstinate moods, Bobby fought back, whereupon George hauled off and slapped him, walking out trailing sparks in his wake.

That night, Burns didn't give Bobby his usual complimentary introduction. Instead, he simply looked at the audience and coldly announced, "Ladies and gentlemen, Bobby Darin." As Bobby strode on stage he offered Burns his hand, but Burns would have none of it. He slapped Bobby's hand away and started to walk off.

Bobby was shattered. Their relationship meant a great deal to him, and now he feared that he might have blown it. He called out, "Mr. Burns, if you don't give me my regular introduction, I won't be able to work."

Burns stopped in his tracks, turned, and looked over at Bobby, who had a hangdog expression on his face. Burns decided to take his case to the audience. "This little boy just lost $2,500," he began, and then recounted the whole story. Afterwards, he asked the audience whether Bobby deserved to be punished or forgiven. The crowd shouted for forgiveness. Burns went over to Bobby, embraced him, and then made his usual introduction. Darin gave a great performance; he never gambled again.

Many performers can balance their relationships with their manager and their agent well enough, but not Bobby. In this case, there was one major stumbling block: Ed Burton and Steve Blauner were not meant to get along. The Csida-Crean organization operated in an almost genteel fashion, careful not to bruise anyone's feelings, but Blauner took the mad dog approach and considered no one but himself and his client. Feelings were disregarded, tempers flared.

Bobby often argued with Ed Burton over the different approaches of the two men. Burton would reply, "We're not in a bowling alley. You can't knock people down like they're bowling pins." Bobby would listen to Ed, nod his head in agreement, and then do what he damn well pleased. As far as he was concerned, his time was running out. As he'd told Nina years before, "Nothing can stand in my way." For laughs, he gave Burton a watch engraved, "Ed—to time the bowling match."

It was only a matter of time before the split came. Ten months after signing with Csida-Crean Associates, Bobby and his lawyer, Frank Barone, tried to get out of the contract. During that short period, Bobby had written and published many songs under the aegis of Trinity Music, for which he received royalties. When the lawyers began to negotiate, it was determined that Csida-Crean stood to lose $100,000 from Bobby's departure. They agreed that until that sum was repaid from the royalties, Bobby would forego his cut. It was an equitable adjustment, considering the situation, and there was no bitterness on either side.

Steve Blauner had already resigned his position with General Artists Corporation and was working as an assistant producer. Now he quit that position too and became Bobby's personal manager. Bobby couldn't have been more pleased when Blauner told him, "You sing and dance and do what you have to do. I'll do what I have to do." Although Bobby made most of the decisions, he was confident that he and Blauner thought alike, and he had no qualms about leaving business matters to Blauner. This way, he explained, "All I have to worry about is performing and creating, which is all I want to worry about."

Immediately, Blauner immersed himself in the intricacies of Bobby's career. They became one person. As the perfect agent, Blauner was rude, crude, impatient, and ruthless when it came to Bobby's interests. He dealt with the accountants, press agents, producers, and record executives and often found himself acting as a buffer between Bobby and the rest of the world. Many of Bobby's oldest and closest friends objected; they were insulted by Blauner's behavior. Blauner regarded even Nina and the family as excess baggage, but Bobby was so excited by Blauner's managerial capabilities that he never seemed to notice.

By the fall of 1958, Bobby Darin felt that he was running out of time. In less than three years, he would be twenty-five. Soon he'd be facing the deadline he'd set for himself so many years before. Even though his career was steadily gaining momentum, he didn't have a second to waste.

Though he was considered the most popular and most critically acclaimed of his contemporaries in the business, he was still classed as a rock and roller, not an adult attraction. "I'm in the worst situation I've ever been in," he argued. "I have a rock and roll hit. This makes me one of a thousand other guys. I have to go beyond rock and roll. I have to prove I can sing."

Accordingly, he decided to put together an adult-oriented hit record, and began looking around for the appropriate material. In April 1959 he was helped by ATCO's release of another single, "Dream Lover," a romantic ballad sung in a more mature style than Bobby's previous recordings. With more commercial momentum, Bobby schemed out the proper package for this new step in his musical career.

Bobby had always been partial to the music of the thirties and forties, to the work of such composers as George Gershwin and Rodgers and Hammerstein, as well as to some of the more recent ballads written by Alec Wilder for Frank Sinatra. Recording this kind of material would be the fulfillment of a cherished dream. Taking his time, he chose the following package: "Beyond the Sea," "Through a Long and Sleepless Night," "Softly, As in a Morning Sunrise," "She Needs Me," "It Ain't Necessarily So," "I'll Remember April," "Some of These Days," "Where Is the One," and "That's All." To these he added "Was There a Call for Me" by his friend Woody Harris and his own composition, "That's the Way Love Is." One final addition was a tune written by Kurt Weill for *The Threepenny Opera*. The song was called "Mack the Knife."

Bobby had been singing "Mack the Knife" in his nightclub routine for almost a year, with only tepid audience reaction. But this was before Harriet Wasser pulled off another coup. She ran into an old friend of hers, conductor/arranger Richard Wess, and she pitched her boy so convincingly that eventually he agreed to work on some arrangements for Bobby's new album. When the three of them got together to brainstorm, Bobby brought up "Mack." Sitting on the piano bench with Wess, Bobby sang "Mack" a cappella using an arrangement he had in mind.

Within days, Wess came up with a treatment so extraordinary that Darin himself was floored.

Harriet's timely introduction of Wess was magical. Bobby called his collaboration with Richard Wess "a perfect marriage," and he would later acknowledge Harriet's contribution by inscribing on her copy of the album, "A little bit of Darin, a little bit of Wess, and a little bit of Wasser." *Bobby Darin: That's All* was set to be recorded in February and released in late March of 1959. It would prove to be a total departure from all Bobby's earlier material, the dynamic leap he needed to break out of the teenage market.

On January 5, 1956, Nina Maffia had given birth to a son, Gary Walden Maffia. Blond and blue-eyed, Gary was a beautiful baby with something of a resemblance to his brother Bobby. With their family still growing, Nina and Charlie were in the process of buying a small home in Lake Hiawatha, New Jersey, when Bobby's success finally hit. Bobby gave them enough money to make a substantial deposit on the house.

Far from huge and certainly not elaborate, the house was a warm, friendly, comfortable home with an immense fireplace in the living room and a knotty pine country kitchen. As a housewarming present, Bobby designed what would later become known as the "Newport Table," a coffee table with a top shaped like the symbol on a package of Newport cigarettes. After sketching his design, Bobby turned the specs over to a carpenter, who then patented the design himself. Newport tables soon began appearing in homes all over the country.

Although Bobby's career kept him on the road a great deal, he remained close to his family, especially to Polly. She missed him a great deal—and envied him the adventure of touring. Her fondest memories were of her vaudeville days, and all it took was the sound of a train whistle to take her back to her days as Paula Walden. When Bobby was traveling, he called her often, and the two also corresponded regularly. Polly's letters were warm and adoring and often included warnings about his health. All were signed, "Your proud Ma."

As plans for the *That's All* album fell into place, the Cassotto-Maffia clan was bursting with anticipation. Polly's excitement knew no bounds. Bobby, on the other hand, drew quiet satisfaction from the knowledge that soon all of his mother's hard work would be rewarded and her dreams for him would be fulfilled. But it was not to be.

On February 10, 1959, while Bobby was in Los Angeles in the midst of laying down a vocal for the album's last tune, "Through a Long and Sleepless Night," a call came through to the studio. Bobby was annoyed at the interruption, but hurried to the phone when the secretary explained, "It's your sister in New Jersey. She said it's very important."

"Sweetheart, it's Mama," whispered Nina. "She's had a stroke. We rushed her to the hospital and . . . and they don't expect her to live." She broke down crying.

Bobby was stunned. His whole world crashed to a sickening halt as Nina's words echoed over the static of the long-distance connection.

"Let me speak to her! Please, Nina!"

Impossible. Polly was in a coma. Frantically, Bobby struggled to think of something—anything—he could do. He remembered reading that the last sense to go before death was hearing, and he pleaded to have the phone placed by Polly's ear. No use. The hospital wouldn't allow any calls to be put through to the room.

"You'd better come home right away," said Nina quietly, and hung up the phone.

The next flight was a few hours away. Lost and with nothing to do, Bobby returned to the studio to finish laying down the vocal. Now it seemed that the violins were his tears. It was gut-wrenching to sing the lyrics:

> *How I wish my heart would leave my memory alone.*
> *Why must I redream, relive the joys we've known?*

Polly had died by the time Bobby returned home. He was shattered. She had given him so much, and he still hadn't properly repaid her. She had been his inspiration, his determination and strength had come from her. Now, just as her dream was coming true, she was gone.

Polly's death also hit Nina hard, and she was incapable of handling the funeral. Wisely, she contacted Bobby's lawyer, Frank Barone, who made the necessary arrangements and specified that Polly be buried under a shade tree, as she had wished.

On the night of Polly's wake, the Frank E. Campbell funeral parlor on Madison Avenue was crowded with hundreds of friends and family. Polly hadn't seen Sam's family since his death twenty-five years before, but even they were out in full force, clutching autograph books as they hunted the crowd for celebrities, watching Dick Clark, Joanne Campbell, Rona Barrett, Connie Francis, and Frankie Avalon file past Polly's coffin.

Bobby remained composed and remote through most of the evening, oblivious to everything and everyone in the room, aware only of his mother, lying in her coffin. He found it impossible to take his eyes off her as she lay there, dressed in blue lace, with her hands clasped at her waist. He wanted to speak to her, to thank her, to comfort her as she had comforted him so many times. But he couldn't. She was gone.

When all but his closest friends had left, Bobby walked up to Polly's casket and gently tucked away an acetate copy of the album he had just completed. It was the album that promised the fulfillment of the dreams of a strong-willed woman from the Bronx and the boy the doctors had never thought would live.

Chapter Five

"I want to make it faster than anyone has ever made it before. I'd like to be a legend by the time I'm twenty-five years old."

— BOBBY DARIN TO *LIFE* MAGAZINE, 1960.

All over the country, disc jockeys began to single out "Mack the Knife" from the *That's All* album for heavy airplay. Before long, record stores began getting requests for "Jack-knifin'" or "Mackey's Back." As usual, Ahmet Ertegun had his ear to the ground, and in another master stroke he had "Mack" released as a single. He expected the record to take off, and he was right. Zooming to the top of the charts, "Mack" held on for five and a half months on the Billboard Top Ten. Even today it continues to sell, three and a half million copies so far. Bobby had made it his own.

Momentum from the single snowballed, and by the late summer of 1959 Bobby was a crossover phenomenon, equally at home musically with teenagers and adults alike. Bobby traveled all over the country that year, drawing crowds wherever he went. On August 12, he made his Los Angeles night club debut at the Cloister in Hollywood.

On opening night, the atmosphere backstage was supercharged. While Bobby made up, spending even more time than usual on his meticulous grooming, reports of ringside illuminati drifted in. Jack Benny, Danny Thomas, Shirley Jones, Louella Parsons, Bob Cummings, Jerry

A typical Darin publicity photo, circa 1959.

Lewis, George Burns, and Gracie Allen were all sitting in the audience. Celebrities continued to pour in: Nick Adams, Shelley Winters, Natalie Wood and Robert Wagner, and even Bobby's boyhood idol, Donald O'Connor. Outwardly, Bobby tried to remain calm and professional, but he knew that on this night, above all, he had to be good. There'd been successes in Vegas and New York, but this was Hollywood. For years, he had dreamed of taking this town by storm, and now he was going to give it one hell of a shot.

A few minutes before the show, Bobby cleared the dressing room of well-wishers. As he waited for his cue, he thought to himself, "This is for Mama."

Out front, the audience was buzzing with anticipation. The room went dark, and then George Burns, ever-present cigar in hand, walked up to the microphone. "I'm very pleased to have been asked to make this introduction. I predicted a year ago that this boy would go through the roof, and he has. He's only twenty-three, and he has a very exciting style. So, here he is, a real nice boy, Bobby Darin."

Cut to black. A thin pencil spot illuminated the backdrop, disclosing a hand holding a switchblade. Then a tuxedo-clad Darin strode out onto the stage and went into a rendition of "Mack the Knife." By the end of "Mack," Bobby had the audience in the palm of his hand. They were enthralled, spellbound. Bobby's repertoire that opening night was a masterful blending of old and new as he sang "She Needs Me," "It Ain't Necessarily So," "Some of These Days," "Lonesome Road," "I Can't Give You Anything But Love," and, of course, "Splish Splash."

Bobby Darin on stage at the Sands Hotel in Las Vegas, 1959.

The evening sped by. Finally, thanking the mesmerized audience for its warm reception, Bobby charged into his lightning fast rendition of "That's All," and then simply walked off stage. He'd given them a show they would never forget.

Immediately after his stint at the Cloister, Bobby headed to Atlantic City for an appearance at the Steel Pier before returning to New York, where he was booked for a guest spot on *The Ed Sullivan Show*. Every engagement was moving him closer to his goal—but the closer he got, the more he was reminded of the very reason for its existence. The specter of a premature death was never very far away.

After rehearsing for that night's *Sullivan Show*, Bobby headed for his dressing room, where he hoped to relax for a few hours. The Steel Pier engagement had been exhausting, seven shows a day for seven days. And there'd be no respite in the near future. The dressing rooms for Sullivan's guests were two flights up, and the elevators were out of order. With more energy than he actually felt, Bobby bounded up the stairs. As he reached the top of the second flight, he saw his three-year-old nephew Gary. Exuberantly, Bobby lifted him up for a bear hug. As Gary kissed his uncle, Bobby started gasping for air. Quickly placing his nephew down, Bobby called for help while he staggered to his dressing room, clutching his chest in pain. Oxygen was rushed in. As he lay there on the couch, breathing deeply into the mask, he didn't seem to have strength enough even to stand up, let alone appear on the show that night. The house physician advised him to cancel, as he was obviously under too much strain. Bobby himself was scared, but he was used to the pains— he'd had them for years and had usually been able to hide them from others.

Sullivan, hearing of Bobby's attack, came to tell him not to worry about the show, but Bobby soft-pedaled the whole incident. He just needed a rest; he would appear as scheduled. Luckily, as the featured performer he wouldn't appear until near the end of the variety hour. The audience that saw him perform "Clementine" and "By Myself" that night was ignorant of the afternoon's drama. Nor did they realize that afterwards Bobby again had to resort to oxygen. After that, it became standard practice for Bobby to carry an oxygen tank and mask with him wherever he performed. The tank remained backstage, easily accessible throughout his performance, a constant reminder that the work he loved so much could kill him at any minute.

Despite the scare in New York, Bobby continued to work at a breakneck pace. In September, he appeared at the Moulin Rouge nightclub in Hollywood and set a new attendance record. In a four-day period, he drew 6,400 people and earned $16,000. *Variety* reported that it was the largest take ever grossed by a performer in Los Angeles. Bobby followed this engagement with his debut as a Vegas headliner at the Sands hotel. There, Jerry Lewis gave him a piece of advice that would, on retrospect, seem more like an omen: "Do you realize you're alone in your generation? Sammy, Dean, and I are all ten years ahead of you. Unless you destroy yourself, no one else can touch you. If you louse it up, it's going to be your fault. Because you have the talent, kid. You're alone. You're alone."

At the end of November, Bobby's leap to stardom was officially recognized by his peers at the second annual Grammy Awards, where he sang "Mack the Knife," which was named Record of the Year. Bobby was also named Best New Artist of the Year. Interestingly enough, the only other entertainer to receive two awards that evening was Frank Sinatra, a performer to whom Bobby was starting to be compared.

After the performance, Vernon Scott of UPI asked Bobby how it felt to match Sinatra's two-Grammy accomplishment. Bobby replied that he wasn't interested in matching or beating any of Mr. Sinatra's achievements. Rather, it was simply his aim to be the best Bobby Darin he could be. Unfortunately, when Mr. Scott's story appeared, Bobby was quoted as saying, "I hope to surpass Frank in everything he's done." Although Bobby quickly and eloquently denied the remark, it is not known if Sinatra ever heard his clarification. Later, when a reporter asked Sinatra what he thought of Bobby Darin, he responded, "I sing in saloons.

Bobby Darin does my prom dates." When that same reporter carried Sinatra's remark back to Bobby, he retorted gleefully, "I'm only too happy to play his prom dates . . . until graduation!"

Through the years, despite a long and close friendship with Frank's daughter Nancy, Bobby's repeated overtures to her father would fall on deaf ears. Newspapers even printed a photo of Sinatra and his buddy, Dean Martin, using a picture of Mr. Darin as a dartboard. Although he downplayed the rift in public, Bobby's rejection by Sinatra hurt him deeply, and only increased his desire for acceptance by the top echelon of show business.

That year, the Grammy Awards had been televised for the first time, and it was certainly a night the record industry took a great deal of pride in. They needed some good PR because such nights were few and far between that fall—the rock and roll business had broken wide open with the payola scandal, and disc jockeys all over the country had been charged with accepting bribes for playing favorites. Many throughout the industry lost their jobs. One of the most thoroughly investigated was Bobby's close friend Dick Clark. "If those bastards give you any trouble, just let me know," Bobby had said at the time. Clark knew his friend was a fighter, but luckily his help was not needed and Clark was cleared.

On December 4, 1959, Bobby himself was questioned by the Manhattan DA's office in connection with appearances on the television and radio shows conducted by Alan Freed, one of the leaders in the rock and roll industry. Alan Freed's rock and roll radio programs had become the model for radio shows all over the country, and his live shows at Brooklyn's Paramount Theater had been sensations. Although Freed was probably more successful than any other man in the entertainment business, he was fired by ABC and WNEW when his name figured prominently in the payola scandals. Eventually, he was harried out of the business he loved so much, dying broken and disgraced. As for Bobby, after his testimony any question of his involvement with payola was dropped.

On November 30, 1959, Bobby received two Grammy Awards, one for "Mack the Knife," named Record of the Year, and one as Best New Artist of the Year. Here, Meredith Wilson hands out awards to Bobby and Van Cliburn.

Payola investigations aside, there were happier moments in Bobby's life that fall. Immediately after Thanksgiving, Bobby's family became involved in a wonderful intrigue. Earlier in November, Steve Blauner and Nina had been contacted by Ralph Edwards, host of the popular television show *This Is Your Life*. It was to be Bobby's night. Nina and Charlie Maffia and their children were brought to Los Angeles surreptitiously as final preparations were made for the live telecast.

On the night of December 2, Bobby was in the studio rehearsing for the CBS television show *The Big Party*, on which he was scheduled to make an appearance the following evening. Suddenly, Ralph Edwards announced, "Bobby Darin, this is your life!"

"I don't know what to say! I usually have a lot to say!" said a stunned Bobby to the effusive host. One by one, Charlie, Nina, Murray Kaufman, Dick Lord, Sammy Davis, Richard Behrke, George Burns, Don Kirshner, and director Norman Taurog all greeted Bobby, who by now had recovered his composure and was thoroughly enjoying himself. He and George Burns even did an impromptu dance. Throughout the evening, Bobby's face flashed many emotions. When Edwards spoke of Polly's recent death, Bobby seemed on the verge of tears. At the show's conclusion. Edwards announced the establishment of a Bobby Darin Award at Bronx High School of Science, a grant for students with exceptional musical ability. Bobby could have had no more fitting gift.

Bobby's acceptance by the media as a major entertainment figure was cemented in January 1960, when he became the subject of a Shana Alexander profile in *Life* magazine. In the article, Bobby was honest about his superstar aspirations: "Right now I could have a roomful of awards and it wouldn't mean beans. I could be the greatest entertainer in the world, and I'd still look at Van Cliburn and eat my heart out—and I don't even know if he plays well. When I've made it, there'll be no more need for the pressure, the yelling, the ring-a-ding-ding stuff. Everyone will say, 'Who's that quiet, powerful guy over there?'"

"Nearly everything I do is part of a master plan to make me the most important entertainer in the world," he explained. "I'm not a spontaneous human being. Show me any top entertainer or top business executive, and I'll show you a guy who has mapped out his life from the very start. I want to make it faster than anyone has ever made it before. I'd like to be a legend by the time I'm twenty-five years old."

The Darin master plan was finally revealed to the general public, with no explanations and no excuses. He did not obnoxiously state, "I will be a legend by the time I'm twenty-five," as so many of the press would later claim. The key words were "I'd like to be. . . ." Nevertheless, the statement in itself would become legendary, and at times it would come back to haunt Bobby.

Shana Alexander had obviously been won over by the Darin charisma. After watching his performance, she commented, ". . . it becomes clear why he has been one of the fastest rising singers in recent years and has earned the right to dream big." She also noted his "practical good sense to look hard at himself and try to understand what he sees."

As the sixties began, Darin's string of record hits continued. "Beyond The Sea" came out in January 1960, and "Clementine" in March. At the same time, ATCO released Bobby's third album, entitled *This Is Darin*, which included such sophisticated material as "Black Coffee," "Caravan," "The Gal That Got Away," and Frank Loesser's "Guys and Dolls." The album was an immediate and resounding success.

Despite these hits, Bobby always found himself on the defensive when it came to his earlier works. Some people, though, were to make Bobby seem more obnoxious than talented. Sid Mark, a young Philadelphia deejay, was one.

Mark, who had a reputation as something of a wise guy himself, was a great Sinatra fan and disliked Darin's work intensely. That winter, Bobby was appearing at the Latin Casino for a ten-day run when a severe snowstorm hit the area, forcing the Latin to close. Each radio station was asked to announce that Darin's show for that night was cancelled. Mark, on the air when the word came down, couldn't resist the opportunity for some sarcasm, and told his audience, "Bobby Darin won't be appearing at the Latin tonight. Someone stepped on his fingers, and he can't sing!"

What Sid Mark didn't realize was that Darin, who was staying at a Philadelphia hotel, was listening at the time. A few minutes later, Mark received a call from someone who told him that Darin would have no trouble getting to his station, despite the snow, and would like to appear on his show that evening. Darin was arriving in twenty minutes.

One of Sid Mark's trademarks was his ability to catch his guests off guard and then attack the flustered victims with gusto. He'd planned his first question for Darin as soon as he'd hung up the phone: "Tell me, if you were at the Latin tonight, who would you be, Frank Sinatra or Ray Charles? Obviously, you have no talent of your own."

Mark never got the chance. Bobby arrived on time and sat quietly until Mark introduced him. Then, before Mark could ask his question, Darin hissed, "Who the hell do you think you are? God? You sit here at this station and make all these judgments!" Still not giving the disc jockey a chance to open his mouth, Bobby snapped, "I listen to your show whenever I'm in town, and most of the singers you play can't even sing on key."

Bobby went on, leaving no space for Mark to maneuver in. The two men then proceeded to hold a two-hour on-air argument. Mark made it clear that he considered "Splish Splash" a piece of nonsense and everything else Darin had done unworthy of note. When they were through, Bobby demanded, "Have you ever seen my show in person?"

"I wouldn't see your show," responded Sid, "if it was the last show in town. As a matter of fact, the only time I *would* see you was if it was the last time you'd be appearing in this city."

"I'd like you to be my guest on closing night at the Latin," Bobby replied, unshaken.

When the evening of Darin's last show came, Sid and his wife had a change of heart and decided to go. When they arrived at the club, Mark gave his name and said that Mr. Darin had arranged for a table. The maitre d' checked his records but found no listing. A call was put through to Darin's dressing room, and Bobby explained that a table next to the stage was reserved for Mark—but he told the maitre d' not to seat the party until just before show time. Obviously, Bobby wanted everyone to see Sid Mark attending a Darin show.

At last, Mark and his wife were ushered to their table. The house lights dimmed, and the show began. After Bobby's first number, he walked to the edge of the stage, stepped over the footlights, and stood on the disc jockey's table, informing the audience, "We have a special guest here tonight, Sid Mark, and I'm going to sing one of his favorite songs to him now." Then he went into "Splish Splash."

Sid Mark, knowing he'd been publicly had, roared with laughter. Backstage, after the show, he and Bobby cemented a friendship that would last for years.

In March 1960, Bobby made his first foreign tour in a British rock and roll package show that also starred Duane Eddy and Clyde McPhatter. He was a sensation, but for the wrong reasons. He disliked British audiences and publicly said so.

Opening night in Lewisham had been a disaster. Bobby, the featured performer, was scheduled to appear last. Clyde McPhatter opened and did his most recent hits. He was followed by Emile Ford and then by Duane Eddy's twangy guitar. The audience, mostly composed of teenagers, was ecstatic.

When Darin made his entrance, the audience went wild. After the commotion died down, he did "Splish Splash," "Mack the Knife," and "Dream Lover." The audience remained his until he went into one of *his* favorites, a slow ballad called "My Funny Valentine." The hardened rockers in the audience jeered and catcalled. "I thought you people lived on the other side of town," Bobby said facetiously to the rowdies. Although this outburst had come only from a small group, the mood of the evening was shattered.

After the show, Richard Behrke, Steve Blauner, and Bobby regrouped to plan on a strategy for the evening's next performance. Behrke felt that "Valentine" should be cut. This was a "rock" tour, he reasoned, and Bobby should give his audience what they had come to hear. Blauner vehemently disagreed. When Bobby began to lean toward Behrke's point of view, Steve Blauner exploded. He had been holding a valise containing all of Bobby's tux shirts. Suddenly, he opened the suitcase and dumped its contents on the floor. Bobby could take the manager's job and shove it, he raged—and then walked out.

Instead of leaving the theater, Blauner took a seat in the audience for the next show. When Bobby's turn came, he opened with the same three numbers he had opened with earlier. Then came the moment of truth. Darin sang "My Funny Valentine." Steve Blauner sat there, still clutching the empty valise, and cried. He knew that this had been Bobby's way of apologizing for the argument. Backstage, after the show, Blauner and Darin embraced. Then, grinning, Bobby said, "Let's go home."

Bobby returned to the States and another record-breaking engagement at the Cloister in Hollywood. That spring, *Down Beat* featured an in-depth article entitled "Bobby Darin and the Turn From Junk Music." Besides extensive analysis by music critic Gene Lees, the article included twenty-nine photographs of Bobby taken on stage during his nightclub act. Lees, one of the toughest and most respected men in the industry, caught the "class" element of the Darin style. "Built on a basic framework of Frank Sinatra, it involves elements of Tony Bennett (an odd kind of harshness in certain high notes), Bing Crosby (a loose-mouthed popping of the consonants B and P), sloppy enunciation, and occasional rock and roll raunch. But there's one big extra: fire. Darin today is unquestionably the only young male pop singer who handles standards with something approaching the polished intensity of Sinatra."

Gene Lees seems to have had a good handle on Darin's style, except for his comments about "sloppy enunciation." If there's one thing that stands out, even today, while listening to Darin, it is his careful enunciation and his respect for lyrics. On the other hand, the Sinatra comparisons were inevitable. Bobby displayed the uncommon showmanship so obvious in Sinatra's work and that same savvy, tongue-in-cheek manner with his audiences. After the release of "Mack the Knife," his arrangements, either coincidentally or not, were often reminiscent of Sinatra's. It can even be argued that Bobby Darin was the only legitimate competition Frank Sinatra has ever had.

Gene Lees and Darin discussed the connection between sex appeal and success in the entertainment industry, a natural topic when skirting

Old Blue Eyes, however discreetly. Bobby asserted: "The sex element is the most important in the business. I'm very self-conscious about my physiognomy. But the fact remains you must sell sex. It must not be conscious, however. You're either sexy or not. There are two types of sex. There's the kind the female sees when she wants to park her shoes under the entertainer's bed. Sinatra has it. Then there is the kind that makes a guy, sitting at a table in a club, say 'Man, this guy is a man's man. I know my woman digs him, but he's a man and I don't have to worry about it because he wouldn't beat my time.' The men in the audience can identify with that kind of entertainer."

Although it is true that he was not classically handsome, many women did consider Bobby very sexy, and there was something about his performances that was very sensual. He'd told Shana Alexander that he wanted to be known as "a singer who moves like a dancer." She'd written, "As he begins to sing, the fingers snap, the shoulders twitch, and the figure seems to grow taller." She'd caught the magic all right. If it is true, as Bobby said, that "there are two types of sex," he evidently had wide appeal. Many women wanted to park their shoes under his bed. Many men just liked his style. Had he not been so appealing, he wouldn't have been such a big night club success.

The previous July, Steve Blauner had been offered an engagement at the Copacabana in New York City, then recognized as the top nightclub in the country. Despite its small capacity—700 seats—a Copa engagement was a feather in any entertainer's cap. But Blauner had turned the engagement down, asking instead for a spot in June of the following year. He figured that Bobby could make a killing with the June prom crowd—and he was right.

Small and intimate was the Copa feel. In the sixties, patrons entered through a long narrow hall decorated in an Art Deco motif of peach and blue palm trees painted over mirrored walls. Ten steps led down to the main room, where a few hundred small tables and chairs were crowded

Classic Darin, circa 1960.

around a tiny stage. Bobby could have had no better New York show-case.

Bobby's Copa act was another masterful mix of old and new. After a simple introduction, he started with a stunning medley of "Swing Low,

Bobby greets friends backstage on his opening night at the Copacabana in June 1960.

Sweet Chariot" and "The Lonesome Road," followed by "Some of These Days" and "Mack the Knife." Patter was kept to a minimum until the second half of the show. Then, during "Dream Lover," he'd focus his attention on one girl, often a child, if there was one sitting ringside. Two more ballads followed, and then it was time to joke with whatever visiting celebrities were in the audience. After the ballads, Bobby would pull out the vibraphones for a bluesy rendition of "Alright, OK, You Win." "It looks difficult, but it is," he often joshed. "By Myself" and "When Your Lover Has Gone" followed, and then he usually sat down at the piano for the Ray Charles tune, "I Got a Woman." With the applause from "I Got a Woman" still ringing in his ears, he would tell the audience, "The album that started the whole thing for us a while back was, simply enough, called. . ." and then he'd charge into "That's All." After he'd finished the song, the stage would go dark, and Bobby would walk off. No encores. And the oxygen tank always got its nightly use.

Bobby was a record-breaking sensation at the Copa, surpassing the draws of Frank Sinatra, Sammy Davis, and Johnny Ray. It was *de rigueur* for visiting celebrities to put in an appearance. Bobby usually greeted his guests warmly and stayed with them a short while before slipping out to his hotel for a rest. However, there was one party of guests that was not greeted as warmly as the others.

Through the years, there had always been a great deal of speculation about the ownership of the Copacabana. Although it was known as Jules Podell's Copacabana, with Podell hosting nightly, it was rumored that the club was actually owned by Sam Cassotto's *compare,* Frank Costello. Costello had heard that Bobby was Sam's son, and, one evening early in Bobby's run at the Copa, Costello sent over a couple of his men. Sitting in the Copa lounge, they told Bobby and Blauner that "the man" was concerned about Bobby's welfare.

"I'm fine, just fine," Darin replied curtly.

Costello was pleased with Bobby's success, they told him. Sam and Costello had been friends long ago: Costello could do a great deal for him now.

At this, Steve Blauner blew up. "If you want a piece of Bobby Darin," he raged, his face inches from Costello's torpedoes, "you'll have to kill two people to get it."

Rising from the booth, Bobby looked down at the two men and quietly said, "I don't want any help from you or your kind. Where the hell were you when my mother needed you? We were broke after my father died. Stone broke. But we managed by ourselves then, and I'll manage by myself now. Get lost."

Bobby and Blauner walked out. Costello and his men never tried to contact Bobby again.

♪

Chapter Six

"I wanted to tell Mama, 'Thanks for strug-
gling for twenty-two years. Thanks for loving
me.' But I never told her."

—BOBBY DARIN TO STEVE BLAUNER, 1960.

Bobby's triumph at the Copa and his successes in Vegas had established him as the fastest rising nightclub performer in the country. The Sands Hotel had been so pleased with Bobby's earlier stint there that they had offered him a new twelve-week deal, spread over three years, in which he would receive a total of $300,000—or $25,000 a week. At the same time, George Burns wanted Bobby back as his opening act and offered him $7,500 a week to return to Vegas with him. Now too many things were happening too fast.

Ordinarily, Bobby would simply have accepted the much more lucra-tive offer made by the Sands, but his personal feelings for George Burns got in the way of his business sense and, despite strong protest from Blauner, he opted to open for Burns. Then things got even more compli-cated.

Immediately after signing with Burns, Bobby was offered a support-ing role in the film *Cry for Happy,* starring Glenn Ford. The year before, executives from Paramount Studios had caught Bobby's nightclub act and had asked him to make a screen test for them. Bobby had eagerly agreed, and veteran film director Norman Taurog had been assigned to direct it. Taurog had given Bobby two scenes—James Dean's opening scene from *East of Eden* and a bit from an old Fred MacMurray movie, *The Gilded Lily*. Bobby had impressed the director with his skills, and Paramount had signed him to a nonexclusive, seven-picture, million-dollar deal.

Since then, Paramount had been out scouting properties. Bobby had done a cameo in *Pepe* after his return from his disastrous English tour, but he wasn't acting, just playing himself and singing a Dory and Andre Previn song called "That's How It Went All Right." He had consistently turned down roles which would exploit his popularity with the teenage set. Thus, when the *Cry For Happy* role came along, it seemed perfect for Bobby's acting debut. However, when production schedules were discussed, it was found that Bobby would be needed on the set of *Cry For Happy* at the same time that George Burns needed him in Vegas.

Because of his close relationship with Burns, Bobby didn't anticipate much of a problem. He assumed that Burns would simply let him out of his contract and sign someone else. Bobby was shocked when Burns refused to do anything of the kind. Unaware that Bobby had taken a $17,500 a week cut in salary to work with him, Burns proceeded to lecture his protege on the rules of the business, lambasting him on what he considered his irresponsibility. "If I were still paying you peanuts and you had a chance to better yourself, I wouldn't think twice about it, but for the kind of money I'm paying you, you have a responsibility to me."

Bobby listened sadly and then told him, "I'm sorry Mr. Burns. I won't do the film. You'll have me in Vegas with you."

Naturally, Steve Blauner was furious when he heard of Bobby's decision. He felt that Burns had been selfish and unthinking, and that Bobby should have put up more of a fight. But Bobby disagreed. "I want to do it because I love the man," said Darin, defusing the argument. As for Steve Blauner, he didn't speak to Burns for years afterward.

This loyalty was a side of Bobby that was not always apparent to the public but with which his intimates were somewhat more familiar.

Although he wasn't always the most gracious of men, he did try to handle his affairs with some sense of integrity and a hell of a lot of honesty, even though this often created some serious problems.

Generally speaking, the American press does not know how to react when faced with total honesty or candor. While a great percentage of those in show business have learned to give the press what they want to hear, Bobby refused. He had been taught to tell the truth and consistently did. He may have been honest about his humble beginnings, but he was not humble when it came to his talent. Reporters and columnists were intrigued and astonished. His somewhat heavy-handed honesty was considered blatantly rude and discourteous. When instigated by a few misquotes, such as that by Vernon Scott regarding Sinatra, misunderstanding increased, and Darin was typecast as an "angry young man." Bobby had never learned how to be subtle. In a world full of press agents, falsified studio bios, and celebrities who would do anything for a line in Hedda Hopper's column, he stuck out like a sore thumb.

And he was equally honest with his audiences. He could not go on stage and put on a false front. If he was feeling "up," fine. But if he was feeling "down" . . . well, that would have to be fine too. Whatever his feelings, they would come across to his audiences. As far as he was concerned, this could only help to make him more human in their eyes.

It was this same steadfast honesty that endeared him to his friends, especially those from his earliest days. His friendship with Dick Lord, as well as with Harriet Wasser, Rona Barrett, George Scheck, and Richard Behrke, continued until his death. After his initial success, he gave Ellen and Dick Lord and Mickey and Richard Behrke white convertibles.

Bobby had been best man at the Behrkes' wedding, and the car was their wedding gift. When Bobby pulled up in front of their apartment, he danced and sang in the street all around the car to get their attention. The Behrkes were touched; "Bobby, are you crazy? You get thousands of dollars to perform, and here you are doing it for nothing in the street." He didn't care, he was so excited that he could share his success with the people he loved.

Richard Behrke was, incidently, the perfect example of the kind of loyalty Bobby received back. During their Sunnylands day, Behrke played the trumpet, but a few years later, when he realized that Bobby was going to be a success in the music industry, Behrke took piano lessons so he could act as Bobby's conductor and accompanist. Bobby paid him less in this position than Behrke could have gotten from anyone else, but he remained with Darin for as long as Bobby wanted him.

After the *Cry For Happy* mix-up with Burns, Bobby was upset and confused. Publicly, he was fatalistic about this loss of the role. "Had it been meant to happen," he stated, "then it would have." But the fact was that he was sinking into a deep depression. Being a motion picture actor had been a dream for years. He had come so close, only to see one of those he loved most cause the opportunity to slip away.

In this frame of mind, Bobby opened at the Three Rivers Inn in Syracuse, New York. As usual, his inner attitudes were reflected in his moods, and his first two shows were remarkably lackluster. Bobby was performing in a zombie-like trance, sometimes talking more than he was singing. After the third straight night of tepid performances, Blauner went to Darin's dressing room and confronted him. His shows were listless, he was cheating the audience.

"Maybe I should quit the business," Bobby replied in a daze. "There's no one left for me to love," he continued, near tears. "No one. There's no one for me to prove anything to. Mama's dead. Mr. Burns couldn't care less about me. What's left?"

"I wanted . . . I wanted to tell Mama, 'Thanks for struggling for twenty-two years. Thanks for loving me.' But I never told her. She never knew how much I . . . how much I loved her . . . appreciated her."

Steve tried to calm him down. "Take a vacation," he suggested. "Get some rest. Make the film. You don't have to go to Vegas with Burns; he doesn't even have a signed contract."

Bobby just shook his head. "I'll go to Vegas. I still love that man."

Two hours later, Bobby was back on stage and, for some reason, the

Inn was not as crowded as usual, which didn't help Bobby's mood at all. He started his first song, then stopped abruptly and tried to tell some jokes. When they failed to get much response, he began to talk. Looking out at the audience, he told them, "I did a bad thing. I drilled holes in the floor of the club, and it's slowly sinking."

The audience didn't know whether to laugh or not. "See, some nights you come out and you feel like 'Let's sing!' But other nights, well, it's really disheartening for an entertainer to walk out to empty tables."

The silence was deadly. Even the clink of glasses had ceased. Waiters stood still, silently watching Bobby, trying to determine what was going on.

Bobby rambled on, almost arrogantly, "When I come out and sing the first few bars of Bill Bailey . . . well, it's very exciting. Well . . . tonight it hasn't been. I'd like to sing more for you tonight, but I can't. I'm just a little bit out of spirit. Maybe you came in here thinking to yourself, 'He's supposed to be a conceited kid, he's supposed to be arrogant.' Well, it isn't so. Any fool knows that bravado is always a cover-up for insecurity. That's the truth. And on that note, I'll say goodnight. God love you."

Then he walked off the stage.

Despite his professed cynicism and worldliness, Bobby Darin seemed to need to be in love. Since his first devastating love affair, when he was only nineteen, he had gone through a series of relationships, some more serious than others. One of the earliest, of course, had been with Connie Francis. After their break-up, there was a quick succession of romantic entanglements. For a short period of time, Bobby was seen escorting actresses Cara Williams and Judi Meredith to various nightspots. Then there was a somewhat more serious but still brief affair with singer Keeley Smith. However, none of these women—or any of the half dozen others Bobby saw in this period—were looking for a permanent relationship, and Bobby was. Marriage and a family meant a great deal to him, and both were included in his plans. As with everything else, he didn't have time to waste on meaningless romantic interludes.

Bobby and JoAnne Campbell host a table of friends at the Copa. *From left to right:* Harriet Wasser, Judy Tannen, Dick Lord, Ellen Lord, Bobby and JoAnne, Nina Cassotto, Richard Behrke, Steve Karmen, and Richard Wess with an unidentified date.

In late 1958, while appearing in an all-star rock and roll show, Bobby met a young singer named Joanne Campbell. Joanne had been a drum majorette back home in Jacksonville, Florida, and had toured with the USO as a dancer before trying her hand at singing. In 1957, she had recorded a song entitled "Come On, Baby" for Eldorado Records, and it was something of a hit. Allan Freed showcased her at the Apollo in Harlem, and then featured her at the Brooklyn Fox. It was there that Bobby met and fell deeply in love with this tiny, beautiful, blonde girl. He was ecstatic. Writing to Richard Behrke at the time, he announced, "Get ready for this one! I think I've flipped over a little girl named Joanne Campbell. Don't break up—she's sweet, adorable, and I don't know . . . I just love being with her. I think it's mutual."

Soon, Bobby and Joanne were seeing a lot of each other. Though both were heavily involved in careers that often kept them on the road, they managed to spend time together. If in New York, it was at Joanne's apartment. More often than not, however, Bobby was exhausted. Although Joanne might have planned these quiet evenings around soft music and candlelit dinners, they seldom turned out that way. Soon after arriving, Bobby would usually fall asleep on the couch. Joanne would sit, Bobby's head resting in her lap, watching television and watching the candles melt.

By the spring of 1960, their relationship had reached a crucial point. Bobby wanted to get married, but Joanne was undecided. Her singing meant a great deal to her, and she questioned her ability to divide her attention between Bobby and her career. At one point, she sought Nina's advice. Nina was very fond of Joanne, as were the rest of Bobby's family, but nevertheless she warned Joanne that unless she was willing to subordinate her own interests to Bobby's, to give him the kind of home *he* wanted, the marriage would never work. Bobby had been the center of attention for too long to suddenly share the spotlight with anyone else. After carefully considering all of their options, Joanne and Bobby finally decided that it was best to break up. At the time, Joanne told the press, "I love Bobby very much, but he wants me to give up my career and be a housewife—and I just can't do that right now." It took Bobby almost six months to recover.

Chapter Seven

*"You should know what some people have to
face every day of their lives, the fight they
have to put up just to stay alive."*
—Bobby Darin to Sandra Dee, 1961.

In the late summer of 1960, Bobby was given his first real movie role, the fourth lead in *Come September*. It was a good part, that of a college boy visiting Italy for the summer who meets, romances, and falls in love with another American tourist, played by Sandra Dee. The cast also included Rock Hudson and Gina Lollobrigida.

When Bobby arrived on location in Portofino, Italy, he was still hurting from his aborted romance with Joanne Campbell. It was only natural, then, for him to be attracted to Mary Douvan, a beautiful woman with dark hair and white skin, a veritable china doll who looked much younger than her thirty-nine years. She was in Italy acting as chaperone to her daughter, Sandra Dee. Although Bobby's preliminary moves in Mary's direction were well received, his attentions were eventually redirected toward her daughter. Mary was not happy about this.

At eighteen, Sandra Dee's beauty was infused with such irresistible innocence that the combination knocked Bobby for a loop. She was born Alexandra Zuck on April 23, 1942, and was of Russian descent. Her parents separated when she was very young. As a child, Sandy had become a successful model. In 1957, at the age of fourteen, she made her motion picture debut in *Until They Sail*. Following this with a string of film successes such as *The Reluctant Debutante, Imitation of Life, Gidget, A Summer Place, Portrait in Black, Romanoff and Juliet,* and *Tammy Tell Me True,* she had quickly become one of the top motion picture actresses in the country. Although she would forever be identified with the roles of Gidget and Tammy, she had shown fine dramatic skills in *Imitation of Life* and *Portrait in Black.* However, she understood that it was the light comedy roles at which she excelled, and it was these she concentrated on. By the time she was appearing in *Come September,* she was already one of the top box office attractions in the country.

For all her motion picture sophistication, Sandy was still very much a little girl at heart. The few dates she had been on had been more for publicity than romance. On the whole, her personal life was almost nonexistent; she lived in a world of interviews, photo sessions, fashion layouts, and sound stages. The most important priorities she had were keeping her figure slim and her smile bright so that Alexandra Zuck could continue to present to her public the image of "Sandra Dee, Movie Star." It is a testimony to both Sandra and her mother that in the midst of Hollywood's shallow lifestyle, Sandy had managed to retain the wide-eyed innocence she epitomized so well.

In a very short time, Bobby fell madly, passionately in love with her, and Sandy, in the throes of her first real romance, felt the same about him. However, there was one major problem. Sandy was almost constantly chaperoned by her mother. Mary Douvan was not about to have a carefully managed career thrown away, and she did everything she could to slow Sandy and Bobby down, hoping that their romance would soon become "just one of those things."

But Mary Douvan hadn't reckoned with the Darin master plan. Once his mind was made up, Bobby was determined to have this lovely girl for his own. When there were lulls in production, Bobby would spirit her away. "C'mon, let's walk," he'd whisper, and usually they'd wind up in a poor section of Rome or Portofino, where children played in the streets to forget their hunger. Each time a group of children would approach Bobby and Sandy for handouts, Bobby would reach into his pocket, take out all the cash he had, and then divide it among them. He could sympathize.

But Sandy was repulsed by the squalor, the poverty; she'd never seen slums before. Infuriated by her movie star mentality, Bobby would lecture her, "All your life you've been protected from worry and want. You ought to know about poverty. You should know what some people have to face every day of their lives, the fight they have to put up just to stay alive."

Bobby and Sandy relax on the set of *Come September.*

"It was a shock to me," Sandy admitted later. "I never realized how much the sight of two little boys fighting over a crust of bread would affect me. They weren't little boys anymore—they were animals battling for survival. Bobby saw something in those kids that I didn't see."

The romance could not be kept secret, especially on the small set. Soon, items began appearing in the New York and Los Angeles trades. Whenever Bobby would talk to Nina via transatlantic telephone, his conversation would be almost entirely about Sandy and how much in love they were. Nina even found herself going to the movies, just to get another look at Bobby's new love.

Much to Mary Douvan's chagrin, Bobby and Sandy were seriously discussing the prospect of marriage. Bobby's work in *Come September* was completed in early November, but Sandy was needed on location a few days longer. Unfortunately, Bobby had various commitments in the States that made it impossible for them to return together, so Bobby flew home on November 14, with Sandy's promise that she would follow soon. Once back in New York, Bobby told everyone about Sandy and their plans. Nevertheless, there was no announcement to the press.

When she returned from Italy on November 21, Sandy was met at the airport by Bobby, who presented her with a huge seven-karat, emerald-cut diamond ring. Within hours, United Press International and Associated Press announced their engagement to the world. Suddenly, Sandy and Bobby had become America's sweethearts. Sandy announced to the press that they would not be wed until she completed production of her next film, *Tammy Tell Me True*, which she was to start on December 17. However, plans were already in the works for the marriage to take place on December 2 at the Cassotto home in Lake Hiawatha. Mary Douvan was furious at Bobby and Sandy for making such plans despite her protestations. Instead of stopping in New York on her way home from Europe, she flew directly to Los Angeles, determined not to take part in the ceremony.

During their courtship in Rome, Bobby had talked to Sandy endlessly about his friends at home. He told her how much he loved Richard Behrke and Dick Lord and how important they were to him. Sandy was petrified. She had to make a good impression on Bobby's friends; if she didn't, she was afraid she might lose him. Bobby, on the other hand, had no fears at all. He was so thrilled with Sandy and so madly in love with her that he couldn't wait to introduce her to the Lords and the Behrkes. On the way home from the airport, Bobby took Sandy to the Lords' apartment.

Dick Lord was out and Ellen was cleaning when she heard a commotion in the street. Then, before she could see where the noise was coming from, someone rang her doorbell. Exhausted and not in any mood for company, she looked out the window, calling "Who is it?"

She was surprised to see Bobby standing on the stoop. He yelled back up to her, "It's me and my betrothed." Then Ellen noticed the limousine parked at the curb, with a beautiful blonde peering through the window.

Impatiently, Bobby shouted, "Hurry and open up. We've come to show you the ring!"

Tucking in her shirt and fixing her hair as she ran down the stairs, Ellen silently wished that Dick was home. Nervous that she'd make the wrong impression, Ellen greeted Bobby warmly but noticed that Sandy seemed shy. Once they were all inside the apartment, Ellen saw that Sandy was actually frightened; she barely spoke, despite Ellen's heroic efforts at conversation. Smiling a lot, nodding nervously, Sandy kept twisting her engagement ring round and round on her slim finger. Her fears were groundless. Sandy was wholeheartedly accepted and welcomed into Bobby's circle of friends.

November 30 was Nina's birthday, and Bobby, Sandy, Charlie, and Nina were going to celebrate with dinner and a show in New York. Earlier that day, Nina had been busy making preparations for the upcoming nuptials. All the papers had been filed for the marriage license, arrangements had been made for a priest to officiate, and a very small guest list had been prepared. According to New Jersey law, the marriage license would not become valid until seventy-two hours after it was filed. That seventy-two hours would be up on Friday afternoon, December 2.

On the evening of November 30, Nina and Charlie dressed for their night out and met Bobby at his suite at the Delmonico Hotel in New York, where he was being interviewed by a newspaper reporter. The interview lasted longer than expected, and Nina was becoming impatient. At one point, she managed to get Bobby's attention and pointedly asked him, "Bobby, what time are our reservations for? It's getting late."

"Just a little while longer," was Bobby's only reply. Then he went about finishing up the interview. As he saw the reporter to the door, Nina and Charlie hurriedly picked up their own coats and began to put them on.

As soon as the door was shut, Bobby turned around and gleefully announced, "We're not going to see any show."

Nina usually accepted Bobby's wishes without argument, but this time she protested, "What do you mean we're not going out. It's my birthday and . . . ."

"But Nina, we *are* celebrating your birthday," he said, eyes gleaming devilishly. "Sandy and I are getting married. Tonight!"

Bobby explained that the press had heard of the original wedding plans and that he and Sandy didn't want the wedding crashed. Bobby had contacted Don Kirshner, and Kirshner was making arrangements for the wedding to take place that evening at his apartment in Elizabeth, New Jersey.

Nina pointed out that the license would not be valid for two more days, but Bobby just brushed off her objections. "Don't worry about that. Donny said he'll take care of everything."

Nina called Vana at home, where she was babysitting with Gary, and told her to take a cab to the Kirshners'. Vee Vee was appearing in a little theater production of *Where the Hell Is Fifi?* in New York, but she too was called and managed to head for Donny's. Then Bobby, Sandy, Nina, and Charlie were off to the Kirshners' themselves.

Once they were there, all hell broke loose. Donny hadn't done anything about the license. Nina stifled the "I told you so" urge and took matters into her own hands. In a short time, she had the name and telephone number of a judge in Parsippany, the one man who could waive the seventy-two hour ruling. By then it was eleven o'clock. It took a great deal of prodding on Nina's part before the judge's wife would awaken her husband. Once she had the man's ear, she talked a blue streak. "This isn't just any couple. They're very busy, and they both have commitments in other cities tomorrow. There have to be exceptions sometimes." Eventually, the judge agreed to sign the license.

At this hour, Bobby, Sandy, Nina, and Charlie jumped in a limousine and rushed to the judge's home, where he greeted them in bathrobe and slippers. He was just as anxious to go back to bed as Sandy and Bobby were to get married, and the papers were signed quickly.

Back they went, into the limo, but on the return trip to Donny's apartment they noticed that they were being followed. "Lose that car," Nina shouted to the driver. No use. Then Nina recognized their pursuer as the father of a friend of Vana's. Finally, she told their own chauffeur to pull over to the side so that she could talk to him.

The man explained that he had heard about the wedding through the cab driver who had taken Vana to the Kirshners'. He was a professional news photographer and hoped to get some exclusive pictures. Nina tried to explain the situation, "They really don't want any publicity; they don't want any photographers around. Please understand. They just want to keep this their own secret for a while."

But the photographer insisted, loath to pass up this golden opportunity. "Just one picture, and I'll get lost. Please, just one," he pleaded.

Though Bobby and Sandy were exhausted, they agreed—as long as they could get it over with quickly. There on the road, in the back of the limousine, Bobby and Sandy posed for the one photograph that would capture their wedding for the public.

Finally, all the technicalities were taken care of. At three in the morn-

Newlyweds Bobby and Sandy in an airplane, circa 1960.

ing on December 1, with a plain gold wedding band borrowed from Don Kirshner's father-in-law, Bobby and Sandy were married by Newark magistrate Samuel Lohman. Nina stood as Sandy's maid of honor, and Richard Behrke was Bobby's best man. The wedding was attended by only nine people: Richard and Mickey Behrke, Don and Sheila Kirshner, and of course, Nina, Charlie, Vee Vee, Vana, and Gary Maffia.

After the ceremony, hamburgers were ordered in for all, and then

Bobby and Sandy left for the airport. The newlyweds spent a five-day honeymoon in Los Angeles before flying back to the East Coast, where Bobby had an engagement at the Latin Casino in Cherry Hill, New Jersey. During the Latin engagement, Dallas Gerson, owner of the club, held a small wedding reception for Sandy and Bobby, complete with wedding cake and photographer. However, after the party was over, Bobby had the negatives destroyed, insisting "This marriage is no one's business but our own." His creative life may have been an open book, but there were moments he treasured which had to be private. This was one of the few.

♪

Chapter Eight

"Never mess my hair."

—BOBBY DARIN TO STELLA STEVENS WHILE
FILMING A LOVE SCENE FOR *TOO LATE BLUES*.

Career firsts continued unabated for Bobby Darin. On January 30, 1961, he made television history on NBC as the youngest performer to headline his own prime-time special. Written, produced, and directed by Norman Lear and Bud Yorkin, "Bobby Darin and Friends" featured Bob Hope and Joanie Sommers. Millions of people finally saw what nightclub audiences all over the country had experienced. There was singing galore, upbeat tunes and ballads, and a duet with Joanie Sommers that featured a long medley of standards tracing the rise and fall of love. Then Hope joined Bobby for an old-fashioned vaudeville routine. Bobby even performed a solo musical skit called "Lucky Pierre" in which he portrayed a Frenchman, an Italian, and an Englishman. He closed the show with "I'll Get By," Polly's favorite.

The trades and *Variety* were unanimous in their praise: "Bobby Darin permits no doubt about his professional standing. Darin works with the aplomb of a stage-scarred veteran." Still it wasn't enough. He had to be a success in *all* phases of the business. He couldn't be just a singer, he had to get involved in the business end of Hollywood, the production and direction end. He already had a hot property—his wife.

In January 1961, Bobby became the youngest entertainer to headline a
variety show when NBC aired "Bobby Darin and Friends."

After their marriage, Bobby took a great deal of interest in Sandy's career. At one point, much to Mary Douvan's dismay, he approached Universal and demanded, in view of Sandy's enormous popularity, that her contract be renegotiated. After some gentle pressure from Darin, Universal agreed. Of course, the fact that Sandy was the top female box office draw at the time (and had been for a while) was a great help to Bobby during his dealings with the studio. He thought, though, that it was his business skill that had turned the deal.

Sandy, on the other hand, had some very definite opinions about Bobby's present and future career and held nothing back in making them known. First of all, she felt Bobby was planning his movie career unwisely. She appreciated his desire to work in serious films, but she didn't think that such work would build his following at the box office. It was the light comedy roles that would help establish him, she reasoned. Once he had his audience, then he could try other things.

If Miss Dee's career were subjected to a careful analysis, it would certainly be true that such a formula had worked well for her (as it had for such others as Doris Day, Debbie Reynolds, Gene Kelly, Judy Garland, and Fred Astaire). Furthermore, although Bobby's work would do much to advance the industry's respect for him, it would do little to further his success at the box office. In contrast, Sandra's career had been very shrewdly handled. Throughout the early years of their marriage, her career continued to blossom as she appeared in *Tammy Tell Me True, If A Man Answers, Tammy and the Doctor,* and *Take Her, She's Mine.*

Come September wasn't the film blockbuster to spring Bobby's film career. He had, however, written the movie's theme, as well as another song, "Multiplication," which he had performed in the film. Released in the summer of 1961, *Come September* was a box office success, even though Bobby's own reviews were tepid. *Variety* pontificated, "Darin does a workmanlike job and gives evidence he'll have more to show when the parts provide him with wider opportunity."

It was a bold move, then, when Bobby, with only two films under his belt, announced the formation of an independent film company, Sandar

Productions, in January 1961. Properties were amassed, and the rights purchased to three screenplays. The first was an original screenplay entitled *The Sounds of Hell* by Richard Carr; Bobby would star in the production. In the second, *Tomorrow, A Rainbow* by Earl Felton, Bobby would play a priest. The third was based on the Arthur Laurents play *Invitation to a March,* for which Bobby hoped to sign Ingrid Bergman in the leading role. The purchase of the three scripts was as far as Sandar Productions ever went.

That spring, Bobby started work on *Too Late Blues,* written, produced, and directed by John Cassavetes and costarring Stella Stevens. *Too Late Blues* was the story of John "Ghost" Wakefield, an idealistic jazz musician who lives in a dream world created by the music he plays. John falls in love with a band singer, Jess. Eventually, confronted by the seamier side of the music business and neglected by Jess, his universe crumbles. Selling himself and his talents for success, he winds up playing a bastardized version of the music he loves. Soon, he is being kept by an older woman and hating himself for what he has become. In the end, he returns to his friends and begins putting his life back together again.

During the shooting, the press speculated on Darin's abilities as a dramatic actor. True, this was a new experience, but after his initial nervousness, everything seemed to go smoothly. John Cassavetes explained, "I think at first Bobby was really concerned that he, as the surefire performer, would dominate Bobby, the creative actor. But it hasn't happened." The infamous Darin ego was kept in check, and the press was off base. As far as Cassavetes was concerned, Bobby was a thorough professional. "If he can come up with something constructive to add to a scene, he does it modestly. With every day he's gaining confidence."

Too Late Blues was almost four hours long when completed, far too long for release. By the time it appeared on screen in January 1962, with more than half the original footage cut out, it was unintelligible. Most critics couldn't decide whether they liked the film or not, and tended to agree that the plot lacked conviction. However, Bobby was consistently singled out for praise. *Cue* commented that "with this film, he is acknowledgedly a good actor"; *Film Review* said, "Darin plays his role with cool authority"; and *Variety* noted, "Darin is effective. His flaccid, unformed face and his fumbling idealism fuse well as he fails to give the needed love to his confused girl."

After completing work on *Too Late Blues,* Bobby had a quick run at the Copa and then went immediately into production of his next film, *Hell Is For Heroes,* costarring Steve McQueen, Bob Newhart, and Fess Parker, and directed by Don Siegel. *Hell Is For Heroes,* which takes place in the autumn of 1944 in Germany, is the story of five men and their reaction to the war around them. Darin received second billing to Steve McQueen.

Late that summer, Bobby began working on *State Fair* with Pat Boone, Ann-Margaret, and Pamela Tiffin. A remake of the 1940s hit, the film also starred Alice Faye and Tom Ewell and was directed by Jose Ferrer. In the film, Bobby played a television newscaster who woos and wins a farmer's daughter. He sang one song, "This Isn't Heaven" and participated in the big production number, "It's a Grand Night for Singing."

State Fair was released the following year. Unfortunately, reviewers spent more time comparing it to the 1945 version starring Jeanne Crain and Dana Andrews than reviewing specific performances. Although most noted Bobby's performance favorably, if briefly, *Variety* commented that the "Remake of [the] Rodgers and Hammerstein film musical [is] too outmoded in style for [a] jet-age audience. Pat Boone and Bobby Darin emerge rather bland and unappealing." Despite these critical notices, the soundtrack of the film, released on Dot Records, was a big seller.

Bobby found the going tough in the movie business. There was a good deal of prejudice against "teen idols" turned actors—and with good reason, since their collective track record was pretty dismal. Bobby realized that it would take hard work and careful planning to establish himself. "If I do really arrive on screen," he admitted, "it won't be because I've got a great set of teeth or a nose that won't quit. I'll have to be an actor, and I believe an actor has to say something. I realize that an actor's first job is to entertain, but if a property that has a message is going to be presented on the screen then it should say what I believe." Despite this realistic appraisal of his situation, Bobby's ambitions remained intact. "I want to do drama, light comedy, the whole range. And some day I want an Academy Award." Sooner than even he expected, Bobby would have his shot.

Stanley Kramer is a producer and director known for delving into unpopular, controversial themes in an honest, straightforward, often emotionally brutal manner. After the completion of his epic *Judgment at Nuremberg,* Kramer chose as his next project a screenplay based on Dr. Robert Lander's book, *The Fifty Minute Hour,* which tells the story of a young psychiatrist and his explosive relationship with a psychotic young American Nazi who has been imprisoned for sedition during World War II. The Nazi—who, along with the psychiatrist, remains nameless throughout the film—initially rejects the psychiatrist's help because he is black. Finally, driven by his own nightmarish fantasy life to the point of a total breakdown, the Nazi begrudgingly accepts the doctor's help. In a series of flashbacks, he tells the psychiatrist of his horrid, tortured childhood and the rejection which led to his hatred of the Jews. In effect, the film—as its new title, *Pressure Point,* indicated—would be a blatant attack on bigotry.

Kramer was in a bind. The role of the patient was difficult and demanding. It required someone who could not only portray the man as a monster but at the same time as a pathetically vulnerable victim of parental abuse. Kramer had never seen Bobby act, but he was familiar with his nightclub work. He had been told that Bobby had a volatile temperament, and he felt that Darin radiated a certain dynamism that closely fit the character. He and Bobby had several meetings, and eventually Kramer decided that "the dissatisfied, electric, catching-fire quality" that Bobby had was perfect for the role.

Later, he would elaborate on his decision to give Bobby a chance at such a demanding part. "I think he was a wonderful actor. I think he felt pain. And when you feel pain and frustration and some failure as well as success, which he had an inordinate amount of, I think those things make a person who has talent a person who has much greater talent. I look at that performance and I think to myself, 'Yeah, I sure didn't make any mistake there,' and however the film may have failed or succeeded, his contribution was major. I can only say I think Bobby touched upon a genius to be able to project his personality into an idea and I'll always be grateful to him for that."

This was the role Bobby had been looking for. And although it was an enormous challenge for an actor as inexperienced as Bobby was, he gave a shattering performance. When *Pressure Point* was released in September 1962, Bobby's review were raves. *Cue* magazine wrote that "the acting is excellent, notably by Sidney Poitier and Bobby Darin in the key roles"; *Saturday Review* commented, "Bobby Darin plays the disturbed fella of Fascist mentality and although his performance is uneven, he has his thoroughly convincing moments." Meanwhile, *The London Observer* stated that "the soft-faced Fascist [is] brilliantly played by Bobby Darin."

Although the film was backed by a powerful promotional campaign ("Some men and some motion pictures just won't conform. Filmed in black . . . in white . . . in rage!") it was a dismal failure at the box office, despite highly favorable reviews. American audiences weren't interested in thinking about painful subjects, no matter who the director was. When Oscar time came around, the film was ignored. This was a bitter blow to Bobby. He knew his performance was exceptional, but apparently the industry felt otherwise. As if to make up for the slight, Bobby was named "The International Star of Tomorrow" by the Hollywood Foreign Press Association at their nineteenth Annual Golden Globe awards in the spring of 1962. But he knew it was an empty tribute.

"Two and a Half Months to Go" proclaimed the headline of the full-page Bobby Darin profile that appeared in *Newsweek* in March of 1962, as Bobby neared his twenty-fifth birthday, his famous prediction still unfulfilled. He hadn't done that badly, considering the 1,500,000 albums and the 2,000,000 copies of "Mack" that had been sold. The $2,000,000 in signed film contracts wasn't bad either. It just wasn't enough.

The hits kept coming, but not at the same incredible rate—a change of fortune that certainly couldn't be traced to any lack of effort on Bobby's part. His material had steadily improved, as had his performance. "Artificial Flowers" and "Lazy River" showed the Darin stuff well. His lyric readings were dynamic, highly charged, and winningly wry. The ad lib "give her the real thing" at the conclusion of "Flowers" makes the song unmistakably his own. Noting "the halfway mark" in the middle of "Lazy River" entices and excites the listener. There was always energy to burn whenever Bobby interpreted a lyric and changed its internal chemistry.

The chemistry was magic on *Two of a Kind,* an album of duets between Darin and Johnny Mercer, composer of such classics as "On the Atchison, Topeka, and the Santa Fe" and "Come Rain or Come Shine." One other album from the period worthy of special comment is *The Twenty-Fifth Day of December,* a nontraditional Christmas album. Arranged and conducted by jazz musician Bobby Scott, it has a revivalist feel, with songs like "Jehovah Hallelujah," and "Child of God," as well as "Ave Maria" and "Holy, Holy, Holy." All classics, all solid work, but rather unconventional. The album didn't sell well originally, but later it became a collector's item, often going for as much as $150 a copy.

Bobby also wrote dozens of songs during this time. One of these, a country-pop tune called "Things," released by ATCO in June of 1962, became a number-one seller. It was released again during the summer as part of the *Things and Other Things* album, along with nine other Darin compositions, including his classic "I'll Be There," which also went on to become something of a hit.

Many performers might have been content with successes like these, but for Bobby they weren't enough. He had been well served by Ahmet

Ertegun, a man he respected and admired (so much so that he even tried to learn Turkish, Ertegun's native tongue). Bobby knew that ATCO had stood behind him and supported him when he needed it most. The five years at ATCO had been busy ones—he'd released an astounding total of thirty singles, out of which he had racked up some thirteen hits. ATCO had also released thirteen albums, most of which had been very well received both commercially and critically. But there was still doubt in Bobby's mind. "Why can't we be like the majors?" he'd ask Ertegun.

Ertegun knew that ATCO was just as good as any of "the majors," but Bobby's question was a sign that he had to move on, if only to satisfy his own curiosity. Ertegun had seen much in his time in the record business, and he took the separation in stride. He and Bobby parted amicably. "You'll always be a part of our family here," he assured Bobby. "You can always come home."

One of the "majors" Bobby had spoken of was Capitol Records, where his old friend and former manager, Joe Csida, had gone to work. Now Csida was responsible for expanding a roster of exclusive-contract stars that already included Nat King Cole, Judy Garland, Peggy Lee, Dinah Shore, Frank Sinatra, Dean Martin, and the Kingston Trio. When he heard that Bobby planned to leave ATCO, Csida approached him. Although Bobby was busily considering offers from all of the majors, including a lucrative Columbia Records deal, old habits of friendship prevailed and Csida won out. On July 12, 1962, Capitol Vice-President Alan W. Livingston and Steve Blauner announced that Bobby had signed a three-year contract with Capitol. At the time, it was the highest-paying record contract with Capitol. Bobby's first release on the new label would be a single recording of the theme he had written for his forthcoming film, *If a Man Answers*.

On the circuit at the Copa that spring, the raves continued to pile up—until three days into the run, when Bobby lost his voice. That evening, Steve Lawrence filled in, and the next evening Jackie Wilson took over.

The press, sensing disaster, jumped on the event and sensationalized it. Infuriated, Bobby attempted to explain the situation to *The New York Post*, "It happens to the best of them. You lay off singing and your throat gets out of practice. No excuses. I blew it. That's all. I blew it." Vocal coach Carlo Menotti was called in, and after two days Bobby was back again, none the worse for wear, his forthright image intact.

As if to prove that his voice was just as strong as ever, on June 21, 1962, Bobby started a nationwide concert tour accompanied by Count Basie and his orchestra. In the two-hour stage show, Bobby sang forty-nine hits and soon-to-be-hits. Reviews throughout the tour were warm and appreciative, but the houses just weren't packed. In Boston only 2,000 of an expected 7,200 turned out for a concert at the Boston Arena. There, matters were exacerbated by a poor sound system. To compensate for the lousy acoustics, Bobby worked doubly hard that evening. The forty-nine songs were augmented by his impersonations, as well as stints on the drums, piano, vibraphone, and xylaphone. The small audience responded warmly, but before the closing number Bobby told them disconsolately, "You should all ask for your money back. This place should be razed."

Bobby's first album release for Capitol, *Oh! Look at Me Now*, was a collection of old standards arranged with upbeat, contemporary charts. Until then, Sinatra had been Capitol's resident swinger, but he'd left Capitol to record for his own label, Reprise, giving Bobby the chance to shine on his own. Still, there was a pseudo-Blue Eyes touch on the cover blurb, "Songs for Swingin' and Lovin'." Each song was special, but one standard stood out.

"Roses of Picardy" had always been Nina's favorite song, and she had been asking Bobby to record it since the earliest days of his career. Bobby had decided to include it as a surprise, and as soon as the album was ready he took a copy to the house in Lake Hiawatha. His eyes twinkled as he put the disc on the stereo and told Nina to compose herself.

"Picardy" is usually sung to a soft, lilting accompaniment, but in this case Billy May had written a big band arrangement, which Bobby had given a jazzy reading. Nina was not amused. In fact, she was horrified. "What have you done to my song?" she protested. "I'd rather you hadn't recorded it at all than to do it like this!"

Bobby was crestfallen. As is sometimes the case, his family could be the worst audience of all.

Bobby was at the point in both his nightclub and recording career where he was considered by many in the industry as a trend-setter. People listened when he talked. As artists demanded higher guarantees, the record companies were passing these costs along to the public. Bobby, sensing the trend, unloaded to a *Variety* reporter in late 1962: "Artists and manufacturers are destroying the disc business with the dickering over guarantees. The industry is more important than the participants, and therefore the participants must work in its best interest."

Furthermore, he denied that his contract with Capitol had included a $2,000,000 guarantee. As he explained it, he was actually a partner in his recording career. He wouldn't make any money in advance; he would be paid solely for those albums that were sold. "A group or an artist," he continued, "shouldn't get his money until the boss gets his. Guarantees should be earned before they're paid out. The artist doesn't take any risk and since the company is taking the risks, it shouldn't pay these fancy guarantees until the artist proves he can line up what he claims he's worth."

Bobby was speaking as an informed participant in the record business, and he was soon to be participating even more fully. Up to this time, he'd had all his songs published by Joe Csida's company, Trinity Music. But in February of 1963, Csida put Trinity up for sale so that he could concentrate on his work at Capitol. To protect his interests, Bobby purchased the company and installed Ed Burton as executive vice-president and general manager. For $350,000, Bobby was in a position to be fully involved in all facets of the music business.

At first, he maintained a low public profile, locating the Trinity office at Sixth Avenue and Fifty-Fifth Street. A short while later, he ensconced himself in comfortably modern surroundings in the Brill Building at Broadway and Forty-Ninth Street. His executive suite was dark paneled, furnished with tan carpets and black leather furniture. One wall was totally occupied by a black lacquered Chinese bookcase with the latest audio equipment built into it.

The first six months were spent learning the ins and outs of the company and the publishing industry. After all, whatever Bobby chose to do was going to be done right. Trinity Music couldn't be a half-baked effort if it was going to be the best in the business. And the best was all that Bobby was interested in.

♪

Chapter Nine

*"You could always tell who really loved Bobby
the most or who he loved the most because,
without fail, these were the people he would
hurt. If he loved you, he had to hurt you."*
—VEE MAFFIA TO AUTHOR, 1979.

Immediately after their marriage, Bobby and Sandra moved into their
first home, a large Tudor place on Stone Canyon Road in Bel Air. From
the beginning, Bobby made it very clear that his home life and his marriage were no one's business but his own. The destruction of the wedding pictures was a case in point.

Hollywood was under the velvet-gloved, iron-fisted tyranny of
Louella Parsons and Hedda Hopper, and Bobby's abrasive methods of
protecting his privacy set tongues wagging. All requests for interviews
and photos were turned down, a tactic which certainly didn't help
Sandy's career. Sandy was upset by this, but Bobby countered more than
once, "If we let them in the front room, then they'll want to shoot the
bedroom, and before we know it, they'll have me in the tub with you
scrubbing my back for them." Eventually, Sandy learned to live with
Bobby's attitude, but she did so begrudgingly.

All in all, she found life with Bobby Darin a somewhat intimidating
experience. He was intelligent, God knows, and strongly opinionated. At

Bobby and Sandy at the Academy Awards in April 1961, their first public appearance as man and wife.

one point, she admitted, "Bobby petrifies me. Sometimes I just sit and look at him in awe." Studio flacks, publicists, and hairdressers, her career's companions, were never like that.

Sandra Dee had always been known for her bubbly, effervescent personality, but early on in the marriage she had lost much of that in Bobby's company. "I've discovered," she explained, "that when you love someone, there are times when you don't know what to say." Bobby had to make adjustments too, but they were the kind that displeased his friends. The "movie star" and the "nightclub singer" were not the best of soulmates, especially when the "movie star" hated the nightclub life and wanted no part of it.

One evening, when Bobby was appearing at the Three Rivers Inn, he invited his entourage back to his suite, where Sandy was waiting. As usual, he was "up" from the performance and needed time to get unwound. Sandy, on the other hand, had been drinking and was looking for an argument. When Charlie Maffia, Dick Lord, and Steve Blauner appeared at the door, she was furious.

Bobby was in the kitchen fixing a spaghetti dinner when Sandy began harping about Blauner. "When he says 'bend your knee,' you bend your knee," she goaded. "You're his puppet."

Bobby ignored the remark. He had heard it all before. Sandy, not getting any satisfaction from Bobby, turned on Steve. "I signed two hundred autographs today," she bragged. "How many did Bobby sign?"

Blauner usually held his tongue when Sandy was in one of her moods, but this time he was fed up. "What you don't realize, Sandy," he shot back, "is that it's not how many autographs you signed today but how many you'll be asked to sign five years from today." A hush fell over the room as Blauner picked up his coat and left. But Sandy wasn't through.

"You care for your friends more than me," she mumbled.

"You're being tiresome, Sandra," Bobby replied, "and I really don't feel like going into this."

"Why do you need them around us all the time?" she whined. "Can't we have some time alone? I married you, not them!"

"God damn it, I'm warning you! Shut up!" Bobby felt he was losing control.

"Do you think this is fun for me?" she persisted doggedly. "I hate this life! Every night I have to sit there and watch your show, night after night, that's all I do!"

Bobby steamed silently as Sandy, who knew better, continued. "I think Blauner only stays around because he's in love with you." Sandy had done the unforgivable—she had insulted one of Bobby's friends. The color drained out of his face. Before anyone knew what was happening, he had slapped her hard. She sank to the floor in tears.

Bobby knelt beside her, tears welling up in his eyes. "If you ever say that again," he told her, "if you ever insult my friends like that again, I don't know what will happen to us."

The next afternoon, Bobby and Dick Lord were outside grilling hot dogs for a barbecue. Mentioning a particularly attractive girl who was staying at the Inn, Bobby asked Dick, "If I told you that she was in Room 303 waiting for you, would you go up?"

Dick Lord looked at Bobby, a puzzled expression on his face. "What kind of question is that? Here we are making hot dogs and you ask me a question like that."

"I was just thinking," Bobby explained, "that I wouldn't do it because I really love Sandy so much."

There were other areas where Sandy and Bobby's divergent wills clashed. It was patently obvious from the beginning that Sandy hated most of Bobby's friends. It was all she could do to tolerate them. She refused to compromise, and eventually Bobby realized that if he didn't accept her lifestyle as his own, he would lose her. So he tried to change and threw himself into a stereotypical Hollywood existence. He saw his old friends less frequently, and they felt betrayed and discarded, though they understood who was behind it all.

Despite these crucial warning signs, Bobby and Sandy were determined to make their union work. When Sandy became pregnant in March 1961, they were ecstatic. Sandy carried well and had an easy, relatively untroubled pregnancy.

While awaiting the event, Bobby very vocally advocated natural childbirth, while Sandy resisted his suggestion. Finally, on December 16, Sandy was taken to Cedars of Lebanon Hospital in Los Angeles. Now Sandy decided that she wanted to have the baby naturally, with Bobby by her side in the delivery room. But when the doctor gave Bobby the news of Sandy's change of heart and asked him to wash up, he panicked. "I can't do it, Doc. I can't go in there and see her in all that pain!" Sandy had her baby alone. So much for the dreams and realities of parenthood.

"You have a healthy Russian peasant for a wife. She can have plenty of children," said the doctor who delivered the six-pound, eight-ounce boy. They decided to call the baby Dodd, the name Bobby's nurses had given him, but the closest the Russian Orthodox Church could come with a christening name was the Russian "DaDa." A few weeks later, the child was rechristened Dodd Mitchell at Saint Anne's Episcopal Church in the Bronx, with Charles Maffia and Olga Duda, Sandy's aunt, in attendance as godparents.

A month before Dodd's first birthday, the Hollywood press started its counterattack against Bobby. "Darin-Dee Break Up" headlined the February 1962 issue of *Movie TV Secrets*. "Bobby Darin and Sandra Dee Hurl $2 Mil Suit at Fan Mag" headlined the February 15, 1962, edition of *Daily Variety*. Only thirteen months after their marriage, Bobby and Sandy were already victims of the Hollywood rumor-mongers. Since Bobby had shut them out, the press started manufacturing their own quotes and notes—such as the story with the headline "The Terrible Truth About Sandra Dee's Baby," which upon investigation turned out to be a truth no more terrible than that Bobby refused to allow his son to be photographed by the press.

In the lawsuit against Countryside Publications, publishers of *Movie TV Secrets,* the couple alleged that the article had damaged their reputation and was a "false and highly fictional account of their lives" which had been "quiet and exemplary" since their marriage. "Furthermore," Bobby told the press, publications like *Movie TV Secrets* were "a paper form of degeneracy. They present fiction to a group of minds who are not aware that it is fiction." Photographers were also to blame. "There are certain times that I don't want my picture taken. If my wife's stepping out of a car and it looks like it's going to come out an indecent picture, don't I have a right to object?"

Although the article in question was totally fictitious and the Darin marriage was basically peaceful, Sandy's hatred of Bobby's nightclub career continued to eat into the basis of the union. Bobby was happiest when he was onstage, and it was at this time that Sandy would do her best to make him miserable.

Bobby's hair had begun to thin noticeably by his early twenties. It was a problem he was very sensitive about, and he spent thousands of dollars on toupees. Sandy was well aware of her husband's vanities and did her best to use them to her own advantage. Often, standing backstage with Bobby before a show, she would look him straight in the eye, in her most studied wide-eyed sincerity, and say, "My God, Bobby, you're not going on with your toupee like that, are you? It's crooked." With this, Bobby would rush back to his dressing room, just as the orchestra was sounding his cue. The toupee never needed any adjustment. Or Sandy would unload one for guilt's sake. "I just don't know what to do; the baby is sick," she'd say, just before he went on. Somehow, he never allowed it to interfere with his performance.

Eventually, but inevitably, by March of 1963, the fan magazines' overzealous predictions had come true. The Dee-Darin marriage was in trouble. On March 27, columnist/reporter Harrison Carrol printed the terse Universal Studios press release: "Sandra Dee and Bobby Darin have separated. Sandra will remain in the family home."

Now it was obvious to all that despite Bobby and Sandy's love for each other their careers and personalities were not compatible. Both were heartbroken over the breakdown in their relationship and hoped that a brief separation would help clear the air. But it would be only the first of many trial separations.

After a few weeks, they got back together again. Sandy agreed to try her hardest to leave "Sandra Dee, Movie Star" at the studio and be Sandra Cassotto at home. For his part, Bobby agreed to suspend his lucrative nightclub career by the end of the year in order to be home more often. And for a time the reconciliation seemed to work. Often they would ride horses by the beach or indulge in one of their greatest loves, marathon sessions of board games. They played everything—Monopoly, Careers, Life, Clue, and Yahtzee were among their favorites. They were happy just spending hours together at home, alone with Dodd, entertaining themselves.

Although they were both basically homebodies, Sandy especially did not enjoy going out to premieres or Hollywood parties. Bobby craved his idyllic personal life, but he still had to put in appearances at industry functions. Often, Bobby and Sandy would be committed to going somewhere and at the last minute they would back out: Sandy had a headache or maybe Dodd was sick. They seldom entertained during their marriage and when they did Sandy would usually excuse herself before the evening's end.

Sandy's attitude was difficult for Bobby, who enjoyed sharing his home with friends and acquaintances in the business. On the other hand, it shouldn't be assumed that Sandy was the only problem in the marriage. Bobby could be very difficult to live with. He was a perfectionist on stage and at home; his various careers put him under considerable physical strain, and he'd often become short-tempered and impatient. For him, career and home were one and the same. Sandy was used to being the prima donna, and Bobby indulged her often. When he'd draw the line, wills clashed and fireworks flew. And when Bobby was looking for a fight, he wouldn't quit until he provoked one.

The months passed, and the ups and downs in the Darin-Dee marriage continued. Bobby found himself in a professional and personal quandary, but he was trying to do the right thing. He told Louella Parsons, "At this particular moment in my life my family comes first. Maybe that's what makes me different from other guys. Sure my career means a hell of a lot, but it will never come before Sandy and my son. What could possibly be more important than a man's family?"

How long could this go on?

Despite his heavier commitments to Capitol Records and to his own music publishing company, Bobby's interest in film remained strong. The role in *Pressure Point* had opened agents' eyes, and offers started flooding in. His problems with Sandy had led to a reconsideration of his priorities, and he made an effort to keep his work closer to home and family. Film work seemed the natural solution—especially if it was a project he could share with Sandy.

Bobby and Sandy thoroughly enjoyed working together, and the pro-

The RKO Palace Theater marquee, on Seventh Avenue in New York City,
starring Dee and Darin in *If a Man Answers*, November 1962.

duction of *If a Man Answers* seems to have held no problems. They arrived at the studio together each morning, were made up together, and shared the same specially designed dressing room suite. They were totally supportive of each other and were always on the set for the other's scenes, whether they were needed or not. On his own, though, Bobby was in his element, known as an actor who would take chances and perform under difficult circumstances.

After completing *If a Man Answers*, Bobby began work on *Captain Newman, MD*, a wry and touching antiwar drama about a psychiatrist charged with patching up shell-shocked soldiers and returning them to the front. Bobby was given the role of Corporal Jim Tompkins, a much-decorated flyer who cracks up, questioning his bravery after he has failed to save a friend from a burning plane. Director David Miller saw in Darin the same vulnerable qualities that had intrigued Stanley

Kramer. "The part needed a difficult personality with a chip on his shoulder," Miller recalled. "Bobby had a reputation as an angry young man. His image seemed to fit all the prerequisites. It seemed many people didn't like him, and I couldn't find out why. When I met him, he was so much more than I expected. I just fell in love with him." The fact that both Bobby and Jim Tompkins were high-strung, volatile personalities made Darin's portrayal all the more involved and personal.

On the set, Bobby was all business. Even when he had no lines, he hung out with the crew and was totally absorbed in the process of making the movie. He communicated that interest in his performance.

In Bobby's big scene, Captain Newman (played by Gregory Peck) administers sodium pentothal to Tompkins. Under the influence of the drug, Tompkins breaks down and is forced to come to terms with his inner demons. The sodium pentothal scene would have been demanding even for a veteran actor. But when the scene was shot, the crew was stunned. In a single horrifyingly brilliant take, Darin had recreated Tompkins' trauma, his last mission. One moment, he was shouting in triumph, "Fry, burn, fry, you Nazi, fry!" Then, realizing that his closest buddy had been killed, he wimpered in fear, "God, put back his head!" while cradling his friend's imaginary body in his arms. Finally, he dissolved in uncontrollable spasmodic sobs, pleading for forgiveness for his "cowardice."

Angie Dickinson, playing Newman's nurse, had been silent during the take, but when it was over she burst into tears. Peck was stunned and speechless. Miller had become so unhinged by the scene that he'd fled before the take was over. Composing himself, he returned and effusively hugged and kissed the young actor. Both were trying to hold back their tears.

"Was I all right?" said Bobby after they'd both gained some composure. He needn't have asked.

On March 13, after the film's principal photography was completed, Bobby opened at Harrah's in Lake Tahoe, Nevada. By the engagement's end, he had separated from Sandy for the first time. That same evening, March 27, he was back for an evening airport shot with Peck and

Dickinson, his character's farewell appearance before returning, cured, to the wars. Bobby's emotional state was not helped by the fact that he had a bad case of flu and a 102° fever. Nonetheless, he performed like the pro he knew he was.

If a Man Answers, Bobby and Sandy's film, was released around the time of their first separation. ATCO seemed to synchronize another message to Bobby with the appearance of an album that had been in the vaults for a few years. *It's You or No One,* Bobby's only attempt at LP production, included such songs as "How About Me," "Only One Little Item," and "I'll Be Around." Did he hear mocking laughter in the background?

The world of show business may have had some inverted values, but at least they were clearly defined. Bobby's relations with his immediate family proved more difficult, producing pain and confusion the closer he came to his goal—and the closer he came to the critical age his childhood doctors had warned of. Relations were especially difficult between Bobby and his older "sister," Nina, and her own daughter Vee Vee.

Both Vee Vee and her sister Vana had grown up calling Polly "Mama" and their mother "Nina." Although at first this seemed just a family convenience, it wasn't hard to make the connection. When she was quite young, Vee Vee started to get an idea of Nina and Bobby's real relationship, and this resentment of Nina's preferential treatment of Bobby boiled over in her early teens. During one bitter mother-daughter battle, Vee Vee shouted "Why? Why does Bobby always come first with you?"

Nina attempted to explain, but Vee Vee cut her short. "Don't tell me. I know already," she burst out, forestalling any further hurt.

Over the next few years, Vana also learned the truth, and so did her younger brother. Once, when Gary, then just a child, openly theorized to Vana, "You know, Nina could almost be Bobby's mother," Vana snapped back at him, "Gary, don't ever, ever say that again!" Of course, Charlie had always known. But no one ever spoke of it to Bobby.

None of these resentments ever touched Bobby's immediate world.

Bobby always acknowledged Nina's role in his upbringing, but at the same time he never diminished Polly's. He knew his sister was smart, but he always wondered why she had never made anything of herself. He had no illusions about the rest of his family either. Once he had made it, he confided to friends, he felt that his family was willing to sit back and let him support them. Sure, they had helped him, but to what end? None of them had any initiative, especially Nina, the "Jersey housewife."

As he had been as a teenager, Bobby was consumed by guilt. He wanted to help his family, but if he supported them he'd take away their initiative to better themselves. They loved him in a way that could not be easily repaid in kind. "I can't return that love," he told one of his friends. "I don't know what it is to love the way they love—they would jump off a bridge for me. I can't do that. I can only say, 'I owe you something, I will pay for something.' It's terrible; it's really terrible."

Bobby felt especially ambivalent about Charlie, a good-natured but simple man. Throughout Bobby's early life, Charlie had supported him like a son. It hurt him when Bobby never acknowledged his devotion, when Bobby stated publicly, "George Burns was the father I never had." To compensate for this, Bobby made Charlie his road manager. He'd treat him like any other employee, occasionally ranting and raving like most prima donna club singers—but apologizing soon after.

Nicknamed by Bobby "the great leveler," Charlie was totally unimpressed with the glittery world of entertainment. It didn't matter who you were when Charlie was screening dressing-room traffic. If Bobby preferred to be indisposed, tha was the end of it. Goodbye Jule Styne or Patricia Lawford Kennedy. Once, Abe Lastfogel, head of the William Morris Agency, universally known as "Mr. Lastfogel," begged admittance to Darin's presence after a show. "Hey, hiya Abe," greeted Charlie. Bobby didn't know whether to laugh or cry. But Charlie was that way with everyone.

Charlie was not the only member of the Maffia household on salary to Bobby. After "Splish Splash," Bobby put Nina in charge of fan mail, a position she would hold until his death, sometimes salaried, sometimes

Bobby and Nina, following one of his nightclub performances, circa 1962.

not. However, Nina's employment, as well as Charlie's was subject to Bobby's whims and over the years they were both hired and fired many times. When they were on his payroll, their salaries fluctuated wildly. At one point, in 1964, Nina's salary had dropped from $125 a week to $50 a week.

Bobby's contributions to the family's finances were equally inconsistent. Bobby always picked up the medical expenses for Nina, Charlie, and the children, and he made a deposit on their home in Lake Hiawatha—but he didn't make the mortgage payments. Years later, when the family moved to Ridgefield Park, New Jersey, Bobby announced that he wanted to buy Nina the house as a gift. He put up the deposit and made a few of the mortgage payments, but that was all.

Bobby was capricious in bestowing favors on his family, in mixing his two worlds together. One of Bobby's closest friends in the music business was singer Frankie Avalon, and Vana had an enormous crush on him. For years, Bobby made sure that Frankie called Vana on her birthday, wherever she was. On the other hand, when Vee Vee was studying to be an actress Bobby refused to help her. She had to make it on her own. He wanted no part of anything that smacked of nepotism. For this reason, Vana and Nina were not allowed to be employed by Trinity Music, even though they needed the work. Bobby did agree to have Ed Burton find Vana a job. Anything but typing, she said. So Burton got her a job as a statistical typist, at the same time as he was hiring his son as one of TM's corporate lawyers.

Whenever Bobby was in New York, appearing at the Copa, he expected Nina and the rest of the family to be in the audience every evening. They never had enough money to afford expensive and diverse wardrobes, and often they would have to wear the same clothing a few times with different accessories. Bobby harassed Nina unmercifully about this, yet he knew that her $150 a week take-home pay was totally inadequate to satisfy his own need to exhibit the perfect family.

He never could see them as they were, never was aware of how others treated them. Steve Blauner was usually rude and discourteous to Nina and her children. Later, when Bobby and he terminated their professional relationship, he simply told Nina unfeelingly, "I'm sorry you had to put up with that, but Steve was important to me professionally."

The public show-biz whiz acted one way, Robert Cassotto another. The "stars" demanded the respect his family never earned. When Bobby

Bobby and close pal, Frankie Avalon, circa 1958.

returned from Italy after filming *Come September,* he brought Peggy Lee and her daughter beautiful shawls. Nina, Vee Vee, and Vana's gifts were large leather bags that looked like feed sacks for horses. On another occasion, Bobby gave Nina a watch inscribed, "To my favorite sister— Love, Dodd." "Gee, yours isn't even gold," said Harriet Wasser when Nina had shown it off. It seems Bobby had given his closest friends four-teen-karat, gold-encased timepieces. Why wasn't Nina worthy of that?

Members of the family were not "friends" for whom he'd do anything. For instance, by the early sixties Harriet Wasser realized that she'd done what she could for Bobby's career. She'd met a young record producer, Bob Crewe, who was launching The Four Seasons, a group she was excited about. Crewe couldn't pay her for her services, but Bobby agreed to help out by keeping her on salary. When Gracie Allen died, Bobby insisted on remaining with George Burns so he wouldn't feel lost in his empty house.

This care for his friends only heightened the confusion and hurt that his carelessness brought to his family. Later on, Vee Vee would succinctly place it all in perspective: "Bobby was like a drug, and knowing him was like being an addict. Every couple of hours, you had to take your fix of Darin, you just couldn't help it. After a couple of hours, you went back for more. You could always tell who really loved Bobby the most or who he loved the most because, without fail, these were the people he would hurt. If he loved you, he had to hurt you. He could be warm, thoughtful, and enormous fun. But when he wanted to be, he could be the meanest son of a bitch alive."

♪

Chapter Ten

*"Somehow he's stronger than any prayers of
mine could be."*

—SANDRA DEE AS BOBBY DARIN HOVERED
NEAR DEATH, NOVEMBER 1973.

It was with a troubled mind that Bobby performed for the crowds at Freedomland in the Bronx on July 23, 1963. He was under the gun—after all, he would soon have to stop touring, his part of the bargain he and Sandy had made to keep their marriage alive. He'd have to fire his old friend, Richard Behrke, still acting as his conductor, and Charlie Maffia, serving as his road manager. He would have no more work for them. Here he was, at the height of his career as a nightclub and concert performer, about to throw it all away. He was not pleased by the step he would have to make.

It was raining very hard that night, as it had been all week. The shows at Freedomland were performed in an open-air theater, and when a stagehand had offered Bobby a large umbrella, he had turned it down, asking the audience, "Who am I that I have to sing under an umbrella? These people are my fans, and if they can stand in the rain to hear me sing, I can stand in the rain. I'm no better than they are!" The audience cheered.

The performance ended and Bobby retired, feeling the effects of his

**Freedomland, July 1963. An engagement that started out as a triumphant
return to the Bronx ended in disaster.**

popular but foolhardy behavior. As he lay shivering on his cot, breathing
oxygen to calm his erratic heartbeat, Behrke walked in with a beef. The
musicians wanted to be reimbursed for expenses, but Bobby maintained
that their performance didn't warrant it. It was a bad time to broach the
issue and Bobby, who was spoiling for a fight anyway, jumped off his cot

and began raving at Behrke. "You're supposed to be my friend! Here I am dying, and you're defending the musicians to me. What kind of friend is that? You want to defend the musicians? Fine. Go with the musicians. After the engagement, leave. You're fired. I don't want you around." His rage unsatisfied, he proceeded to fire the rest of his entourage as well.

Bobby's heart continued to beat erratically, and a doctor was called. Bobby was ordered to cancel the rest of his engagements and return to Mt. Sinai Hospital in Los Angeles for observation and treatment. He was admitted on July 31, officially suffering from exhaustion and overwork, and was released on August 1. He and Sandy retired to Palm Springs, but it was a short-lived retreat. On August 22, he opened at the Flamingo in Las Vegas. Finally, in October, Bobby retired from the nightclub stage. Steve Blauner, realizing that with the end of Bobby's nightclub work his own income would be greatly reduced, took this opportunity to accept one of many offers he had received and joined Columbia Screen Gems as a producer.

From now on, Bobby resolved to devote himself to the nonperforming aspects of the music business. Since his purchase of Trinity Music the previous February, Bobby had already invested $500,000 in developing the business. He had opened offices in Great Britain, Germany, and Australia and had established representation in every major city around the world. TM's catalog at this time had over seven hundred titles, of which forty were top hits. Bobby personally chose songwriters for the company, and he loved getting his picture in *Billboard* and *Cashbox* signing them to exclusive contracts. By the time of his retirement from the stage in October, his stable included Debbie Stanley, Kenny Young, Frank Gari, Terry Melcher, Artie Resnick, and Rudy Clark. And, of course, his own songs were TM property too.

Bobby spent most of his free time at the offices in Nashville and L.A., the latter located in the Capitol Records Tower, right next door to his old friend Joe Csida. "It's the best move I've ever made," he told *Music Business* magazine. "Just call me a family man and an actor who digs his whole scene, side interests and all. Just say I feel mighty good at the ripe old age of twenty-seven."

There was good reason for Bobby's exuberance. TM was hot. Earlier in the year, the company had published both of Darin's hits, "18 Yellow Roses" and "You're the Reason I'm Living." Artie Resnick and Kenny Young had had a big success with a song they'd written for the Drifters called "Under the Boardwalk." Rudy Clark had scored with "The Shoop Shoop Song" and "It's in His Kiss." And Terry Melcher had written two hits for the Rip Chords, "Three Window Coupe" and "Hey Little Cobra."

TM also branched out into television and record production, and Bobby's hand was just as hot in these new ventures. While making one of his last appearances at the Copa, Bobby had walked into the Copa's lounge to watch two young brothers perform. Impressed with the younger, he suggested that he go solo—and Wayne Newton was signed to TM. Not long afterward, a song plugger came to Bobby with "Danke Schon." Bobby turned it over to Newton, who promptly made it a hit and launched his own nightclub career.

It was also through his company that Bobby came to an awareness of civil rights. He wrote thirteen songs with Artie Resnick and Rudy Clark, and a close personal relationship developed between them. But it was with Clark, the only black songwriter at TM, that he spent hours and hours discussing the country's racial turmoil and what should be done about it. Bobby even went on a few marches to Washington, registered as Walden Robert Cassotto, a totally anonymous, totally concerned citizen.

Rudy Clark had awakened in Bobby a dedication to a cause that was to prove much more overwhelming than anything connected with his career. But in those early days of his political awareness, Bobby still thought he could strike a balance—with his career coming out on top. Not even a glimpse of another performer's brush with political tragedy could show him the handwriting on the wall.

On November 20, 1963, Bobby began a week's work guesting on *The*

Judy Garland Show. He had admired Garland for years and had met her a few times in the past. They got along well, partly because of Bobby's obvious respect for Judy, but also because of their similar senses of humor.

Over the previous weeks, work on the Garland series had not always proceeded smoothly. Garland was under enormous pressure to make this series succeed, and her temperament was at its most sensitive. Nevertheless, the finished product each week had been first class, and Bobby was looking forward to his appearance.

Then, on Friday, November 22, the world stood still. Garland was at home when she heard the news of John Kennedy's assassination. She simply fell apart. Sobbing to her daughter Liza, "What are we going to do? What are we going to do?" she rushed off to Pat Kennedy Lawford's house to be with the family. Needless to say, Judy did not show up for that day's rehearsals, or those scheduled for the next day.

The rest of the crew, Bobby, and his costar Bob Newhart had reported for rehearsals, and Bobby couldn't understand why Garland couldn't too. Judy did not return to the set until the third day, when the show was scheduled to be filmed. Although everything went well, Bobby still didn't see how a professional of Judy's caliber could let her emotions interfere with her performance. He was sympathetic, of course, but couldn't ever see himself reacting that way.

April 13, 1964, the night of the 36th Annual Academy Awards, was especially exciting for Bobby Darin. Universal had worked hard for his nomination as Best Actor in a Supporting Role for *Captain Newman, MD*. He was feeling good about his chances, despite the competition from Nick Adams, Melvyn Douglas, Hugh Griffith, and John Huston.

The Oscar competition had much intrigue that year, especially concerning Melvyn Douglas, whose career had begun in 1931 and who had never been nonimated for any award. Sympathy was with Douglas, who'd become seriously ill after shooting *Hud*, the film for which he'd obtained his nod from the Academy. Bobby was still new to the Hollywood game.

He fixed his eyes on the stage as Patty Duke read the names of the nominees. He'd been waiting for this moment of triumph for ten years; it would be the crowning achievement of his career. When Douglas won, Bobby was crestfallen. Hollywood still hadn't accepted him as an actor. At that crushing moment, his successes with Wayne Newton and his own brilliant recording career seemed to pale.

On October 9, Bobby was back on a motion picture sound stage again when he, Sandy, and Donald O'Connor began work on *That Funny Feeling*. Sandy played an aspiring actress who supports herself cleaning apartments. Ashamed of her own dingy apartment, when she meets Darin she has him drop her off at one of her clients' residences. It's Bobby's cue, and the misunderstandings begin. It was harmless fun to be sure, successful formula plotting, and far from Academy Award material. Musically, though, the movie had promise. Bobby and Richard Wess collaborated on the score, with Bobby penning the title tune. "That Funny Feeling" became another Darin original.

Universal released *That Funny Feeling* in October, 1965. Like *If A Man Answers*, it was a popular commercial success, though the reviews were far better. *The Christian Science Monitor* mentioned Darin's "skillful understatement" and "credibility." *Film Journal* remarked, "Sandra Dee and Bobby Darin head an unusually fine cast in this light and breezy situation comedy. Darin succeeds nicely in making the transition to light comedy after his sparkling performance in *Captain Newman*."

The Wess-Darin collaboration produced *Hello Dolly to Goodbye Charlie* for Capitol in late 1964. The arrangements had the same feel as "Mack the Knife" and included popular movie songs, favorites such as "Sunday in New York," "Where Love Has Gone," and "Call Me Irresponsible." Bobby's recording of "Hello Dolly" hit the charts, but never made it to the top. Soon afterward, as disenchanted with Capitol as he had been with ATCO two years earlier, Bobby went back to Ahmet Ertegun, this time recording on the Atlantic label.

Early in the new year, recognition came to Trinity Music. BMI ranked the company as the eighteenth largest of their hundred affiliates and awarded Trinity its sixth BMI Award, given for recordings that have entered the top ten on the charts. The first five awards had been for "You're the Reason I'm Living," "18 Yellow Roses," "Hey Little Cobra," "The Shoop Shoop Song," and "Under the Boardwalk." This sixth award was for Darin's recording of "I'll Be There."

Bobby's talents were employed far beyond the recording industry. He wrote theme songs for two short-lived television series, *Wendy and Me,* starring George Burns and Connie Stevens, and *Camp Runamuck,* with Dave Ketchum. In April, Disney Productions commissioned him to write the theme for *That Darn Cat.* Even the government needed his services. For LBJ's War on Poverty, he composed "It's What's Happening Baby" to accompany a public information film.

Bobby also lent his energies to the civil rights movement. On March 24, 1965, along with Dick Gregory, Harry Belafonte, and Peter, Paul, and Mary, he entertained a mass march in Montgomery, Alabama. The Watts riots in August also made a strong impression on him. Although songwriter Rudy Clark managed to talk him out of going to Watts to appear for the people, Bobby was still being drawn deeper and deeper into the struggle. The turning point came when he started to take notice of Bobby Kennedy. There was hope, Bobby felt, in RFK.

In November 1965, Bobby's weakening heart received another shock. He was in New York taping *The Steve Lawrence Show* and tending to some TM business. Several days before the taping, Bobby had started feeling run down, but he managed to come through the next few days, despite the fact that he was running a high fever. The morning after the show was taped, he called Sandy and asked her to meet him at the airport. "Honey, bring some blankets in the car. I'm not feeling very well," he explained.

All this struck Sandy as a bit melodramatic—until she saw him at L.A. International, his complexion gray, his face swollen almost beyond recognition. In the two weeks he'd been gone, Bobby had dropped twenty pounds. As Sandy helped him into the limousine, he could barely talk. All he could do was shiver.

By the time Sandy had gotten Bobby home and in bed, his temperature had gone up to 103°. Immediately, Sandy called Dr. Levy, Bobby's heart specialist. He advised her to keep Bobby warm and in bed. If his fever didn't break, he might catch pneumonia—which could be fatal for anyone with a rheumatic heart condition.

Early the next morning, Sandy went to the studio to complete sound dubbing on *A Man Could Get Killed*, leaving Bobby and Dodd with the maid. Throughout the morning, she kept tabs on him. Suddenly, in the afternoon, a call came in from Bobby.

"Sandy, I have to go to the hospital. My fever is up to 104, and Dr. Levy doesn't know why."

A thought flashed through her mind: if Dr. Levy had told Bobby he didn't know why the fever was so high, then he must be trying to keep Bobby from learning the truth. Bobby must have developed pneumonia. She tried to remain calm. "Darling, I'll be right there. Just be still."

An ambulance was already on the way to take him to Mount Sinai Hospital. "Meet me there," he pleaded and hung up.

Bobby's condition was grave. At the hospital, Dr. Levy told Sandy that eight of the ten lobes of Bobby's lungs were filled with phlegm. Levy's worst fears were confirmed: Bobby had pneumonia. It was too early to give a prognosis.

Sandy couldn't believe it. In the five years they'd been married, Bobby had been ill countless numbers of times, but he had never seemed so close to death. Of course, she was aware of his fragile health, of the prediction made in his childhood that Bobby would never live past the age of thirty. Now thirty was all too close.

Sandy stayed with Bobby through the night, babying him and praying for him. There was no improvement the following day. Dr. Levy was concerned, but remained noncommittal. Privately, he doubted that Bobby would live another forty-eight hours.

But, almost miraculously, at about midnight on the second day,

Bobby's fever began to drop and he started breathing more regularly. By the following day, he was well on the way to recovery. "Somehow," Sandy thought, "he's stronger than any prayers of mine could be."

When Bobby was strong enough to receive visitors, Vee Vee was ready and waiting—but she was stuck when it came to a get-well gift. Finally, she remembered all those days in his childhood that Bobby had spent recuperating from his bouts with rheumatic fever, days that Nina had tried to brighten up by buying him coloring books and crayons. Bobby, though still under medication, was delighted. "Do I have to color every one?" he asked childishly. Dave Gershenson, Sandy's manager, was also visiting at the time. He couldn't believe that Bobby Darin could become so excited over a mere coloring book.

"What's the matter, Dave?" Bobby teased. "Weren't you ever a kid?"

Chapter Eleven

"It isn't true that you live only once. You only die once. You live lots of times if you know how."

—BOBBY DARIN, 1966.

On May 14, 1966, Bobby reached his thirtieth birday, despite the dire predictions of Dr. Spindell some twenty-two years before. He had built his entire life on this projection and now, for all he knew, the end could be near. Since the age of eight, he had been taking sulfa drugs every day. An oxygen tank and mask awaited him backstage during every performance, just in case. He had had to resort to it more times than he cared to remember. His erratically pounding heart left him exhausted, and it took hours to recuperate from every exertion. He knew that if he continued touring it could kill him, but if he didn't perform that would kill him too.

In a cockier frame of mind, Bobby had said that he wanted to be a legend at twenty-five, and the press had eaten it up. For the most part, they had respected his talent and his need for privacy, and he had endured their questions with fairly good grace. But when the quarter-century milestone came and went, the press started getting on Bobby's case. Now, a columnist for *The New York Post* headlined his column, "Egotist Bobby Darin at Thirty Hits Low Note as Legend," vengefully closing with, "This Saturday is his birthday. It is not a national holiday."

When asked by a more friendly reporter what he hoped to be doing in ten years, Bobby replied laconically, "I hope to *be* forty." Then he detailed his own philosophy, which was tinged with his fears. He had chosen to go back on the road, and he knew the odds. "My philosophy is to take one day at a time. I don't worry about the future. Tomorrow is even out of sight for me. Each morning, I say to myself, 'Well, here I am again! Let's go!' It isn't true that you live only once. You only die once. You live lots of times, if you know how."

Three months before his thirtieth birthday, after a layoff of two years and three months, Bobby had gone back on the road. In January, he had opened at the Flamingo Hotel in Las Vegas. The public saw a more mature, polished, and exciting nightclub performer. After the simple introduction, "Ladies and Gentlemen, Mr. Bobby Darin," Bobby burst on stage, opening with special material that had been written just for the occasion. Sung to the tune of "Swanee," the lyrics started:

> *I've been away from you a long time.*
> *It's been about two years or more.*
> *I've been making some flicks,*
> *But I'd rather get my kicks,*
> *Working this nightclub floor.*

Then he moved quickly into an electrifying rendition of "Don't Rain on My Parade," followed by a well-chosen selection of standards that varied in mood from the sensitive "Once Upon a Time" to the country-style pop hit, "King of the Road."

After a series of impersonations—including Jimmy Cagney, Carey Grant, Marlon Brando, Walter Brennan, Dean Martin, and Jerry Lewis—the stage darkened, save for a pinspot above Bobby's head. The highlight of the show was at hand. He half-sang, half-spoke, "Brother Can You Spare a Dime?" and by the time he was pleading, "Gee, don't you remember, you called me Al," Bobby had brought chills to everyone in the audience. The closing number was "The Curtain Falls."

With this act, Bobby established his supremacy on the Vegas circuit. Until his death, he would remain one of the most consistently successful performers to play Vegas—and the highest paid.

During the Vegas engagement, Bobby hired a young man by the name of Roger Kelloway as his conductor. Kelloway, like Richard Behrke before him, found that working with Bobby could be both very stimulating and very difficult.

"During the act," Kelloway explains, "you had to conduct the band, make sure the timing was right, and give him the feeling that you were feeding him at the same time. Bobby always needed to know that you were looking at him, even if it was peripheral vision; and if you weren't, he'd call you on it after the show."

Kelloway realized that when Bobby was up, working with him could be a great deal of fun—but when he was down, things could get pretty rough. One Saturday, for instance, Bobby asked him to go into the music file and find a particular arrangment of "The Shadow of Your Smile." Kelloway returned empty-handed. "Bobby, I've looked but there's no such arrangement."

"Well, there *will* be by Wednesday, won't there?" replied the boss. When they opened Wednesday, the charts were ready.

In performance, Bobby was a demanding perfectionist and kept on top of everything. After the show, he'd rap it down with Kelloway. "The amplification on the saxes was too high, the strings weren't loud enough, the tempo on 'Mack' wasn't fast enough, and the guitar should be taken out of the second eight bars of 'Once Upon a Time.'" Bobby was almost always right. "He had a great knack for knowing exactly what was right for him," Kelloway noted. "If you gave it to him, if you could keep up with him, he respected you, and he was sensational to work with."

Early in 1966, Bobby signed with Universal TV to do a series called *The Sweet Years*. Taken from an episode of Ben Gazzara's *Run For Your Life*, the show revolved around the trials of a World War II vet who returns to the Riviera after the war to work as a tour guide. Although Bobby was excited about the dramatic potential, the pilot was passed on by all three networks and it died quietly. Movie work shuffled along too.

Early in June, Bobby went into production for Universal in *Gunfight at Abilene*, starring Leslie Nielsen and Don Galloway, with Emily Banks in a supporting role. This undistinguished western was panned by the critics. In fact, it was so bad that Darin referred to it thereafter as "Gunfight at Shit Creek." What good was in the movie came from Bobby's score and the title song, "Amy." For the project, he worked with Shorty Rogers, a gifted arranger with whom he developed a close personal and professional relationship.

Bobby's next film, *Cop-Out*, released in Great Britain the following year as *Stranger in the House*, starred James Mason and Geraldine Chaplin. In this B film, Bobby played the part of a licentious shop steward who fondled pillows, necked with shop dummies, and ran porno shows. Fortunely, he dies in the second reel—and so did the film.

All Bobby's Vegas and L.A. openings were star-studded, but his March 9 opening at the Coconut Grove, celebrating his tenth anniversary in the business, was spectacular. Even Bobby was floored. To his right were Andy Williams and his wife Claudine Longet, Eddie Fisher, Ben Gazzara, and Carol Lynley. At another table were Jack Benny, Johnny Mercer, and George Burns, three of the men Bobby had grown to admire most. Right in front were some of Bobby's oldest friends from his rock and roll days, Pat Boone and Frankie Avalon and their wives. Throughout the audience were scattered such celebrities as Vince Edwards, Mia Farrow, Henry

Bobby Darin as Sheriff Cal Wayne in *Gunfight at Abilene,* 1967.

Mancini, Juliet Prowse, Michael Caine, Ross Hunter, and Nancy Sinatra, Sr. Even Edward G. Robinson was there.

Front and center sat Sandy, dressed in an emerald green gown, a full length white mink, and emerald earrings. Dodd, dressed in a miniature tux, sat on his mother's lap. Both beamed throughout the show as Bobby pulled out all the stops. He closed with "I've Got Plenty of Nothing," to a long and emotional ovation.

More than ever, Bobby knew that this was where he belonged, and he could only hope that Sandy would understand. Sandy and Dodd were the two most important people in his world. He'd do anything to make them happy, but unless he was happy with himself it was all a lost cause—and if he couldn't perform on a nightclub stage he'd be miserable.

At the postperformance gala, a celebration complete with an orchestra and champagne, Sandy, Dodd, and Bobby made a beautiful picture together. But Sandy looked somewhat misty-eyed as she watched her son help his father cut the anniversary cake. She knew Bobby had already made his choice and she could no longer influence him.

After Dodd had been born, both Sandy and Bobby had wanted more children, but when their marriage began to falter they decided to wait until things were more settled. When Bobby returned to the nightclub stage, the relationship suffered. Sandy never liked life on the road. And he couldn't stand her vapid "star's" existence, with its conspicuous consumption. It all cost too much money, and to no end.

The contrasts were overwhelming. Bobby had always tried to broaden his horizons. A voracious reader, he was interested in the outside world. Sandy's seemed bound on one end by Louella Parson's latest column and by the Tiffany store window on the other. Bobby found it increasingly difficult to carry on intelligent conversations with her. She also seemed to be getting too fond of Russian vodka for his liking.

He'd been blinded by beauty for so long. And it wasn't just Sandy's beauty, but that of his picture-book family too—handsome singer married to Hollywood beauty, with adorable son. They had a series of fabulous homes, limitless money, career success, stylish clothes, and best of all, youth. There was no reason why the marriage couldn't work. Both Bobby and Sandy had grown to believe in their image. Eventually, reality had to intrude.

On the morning of May 1, 1966, two weeks before his thirtieth birthday, without the instigation of any particular argument or incident, Bobby woke up, told Sandy he no longer wanted to be married, then dressed and left the house. Although Sandy was heartbroken, she too realized the futility of their situation. She would never be able to deal with his club career, no matter how happy she knew it made him. She

Sandy, Dodd, and Bobby on opening night at the Coconut Grove, March 1966.
This was Darin's tenth anniversary in show business.

had seen the writing on the wall. Whenever they'd spoken lately, it seemed as if Bobby said black and she said white. Their life together had degenerated into a series of niggling arguments, arguments so familiar that they both seemed to know the script by heart. When she agreed to file for divorce, she did so knowing that it would be impossible for her to ever love anyone as much as she had loved—still loved—Bobby.

In March of 1967, when the final decree was handed down, Sandy was awarded their home and all community property (including some oil wells in Texas) save Trinity Music. When she mentioned wanting TM too, Bobby agreed but cautioned her, "With me, TM is worth a million dollars. But if you get it, I'll no longer be associated with it, and without

Rona Barrett and Bobby at a Hollywood party, early in 1968. Their friendship, which began in New York in the mid-fifties, lasted until Bobby's death.

me it won't be worth ten cents. And I'll take everything else." In addition to $2,000 a month in child support for Dodd, Sandy was granted an allowance so that Dodd could travel with her whenever she wished.

Even after the divorce, Bobby and Sandy continued to see each other. Often Bobby would visit Dodd at home and remain overnight, staying with Sandy in the room they had shared as man and wife. "I'm more married to Sandy now than when we were married with a legal document," he told a reporter. "Sandy and I may be divorced as man and wife, but we're still married as parents," he said to another.

It may have seemed a sensible arrangement to Bobby, but for Sandy it was another story. For years after, Sandy would hold on to the hope that somehow, someday, she and Bobby might live together again. Bobby may not have totally rejected the idea, but he dated extensively nonetheless. Sandy dated no one. It was inevitable that she would be hurt, Eventually, she grew bitter toward Bobby for giving her false hopes of a reconciliation. However, at the time of the breakup, she'd confessed, "I know Bobby would have done everything for me. I just didn't know how to handle it."

Three months after the final decree, in June of 1967, Bobby Darin met Diane Hartford, the beautiful wife of millionaire Huntington Hartford, at the Daisy, an exclusive Hollywood discotheque. He escorted her to the Supremes' opening at the Coconut Grove on June 13. Two weeks later, they were spotted together at the premiere of the film *Woman Times Seven*. When Bobby went to London on business, Diane accompanied him.

On August 21, while Bobby was in Paris for the opening of a new Left Bank discotheque, Huntington Hartford took his troubles to the press. He announced that his wife's time was "being monopolized by Bobby Darin," adding that he hoped "she's just having another thing." Hartford was believed to have had investigators following Bobby's every move, looking for Diane. When contacted by the New York press, Bobby stated diplomatically, "She's a charming, sweet, lovely lady, but there's no romantic involvement between us, just a beautiful platonic friendship." Asked if Diane would be joining him in Paris or Monaco, he replied, somewhat coyly, "I don't think so, but you can never tell."

From Paris, Bobby went to Monaco to entertain at and host Princess Grace's Annual Red Cross gala. On August 29, the front page of *The New York Post* featured a full-page photograph of a radiant Princess Grace dancing with a handsome and confident Bobby Darin.

Throughout Bobby's stay in Europe and the months that followed, the press speculated about his relationship with Diane Hartford. Early in

A boy from the Bronx meets a princess from Philadelphia.
Bobby and Princess Grace of Monaco at the Red Cross Ball, August 1967.

September, when Diane filed for a divorce, her husband confidently predicted, "I expect she'll come back to me as she has so many times before." In December, Bobby rented a townhouse in Manhattan, where Diane visited him through the early part of 1968. However, when Diane discovered that she was pregnant, she returned to her husband. The following summer she and Huntington Hartford announced the birth of a daughter, Juliette.

Bobby's life changed radically in other ways after the divorce. As he started emotionally healing, he began to reach out for friendship. When the decree became final, he leased a Tudor-style house on Rodeo Drive in Beverly Hills and reacquainted himself with the joys of bachelorhood. During this period, one of Bobby's closest friends was screenwriter Tom Mankiewicz, son of the legendary screenwriter, producer, and director,

Joe Mankiewicz. Tom and Bobby started spending a lot of time together, talking, watching old films, and playing tennis. As they grew closer, Tom intuitively sensed that Bobby was at a point in his life when he needed a lot of love.

That Christmas, Bobby gave a dinner party for all his bachelor friends. After a full-course feast, all retired to the screening room for drinks and a movie. He'd never been able to entertain when he was married, and now he was making the most of it. "He was so determined to

Bobby and Diane Hartford arrive at a hollywood premiere in his Excalibur, 1967.

After his divorce from Sandy in 1966, Bobby tried to spend as much time as possible with his son Dodd. In this 1967 snapshot, they're shown relaxing at home.

take care of all of us that day," remembers Tom, "It meant so much to him that we enjoyed ourselves and that he had taken us into his home. He was one of the warmest, most affectionate people I've ever known."

As a child, Bobby had never been allowed to participate in sports to any great extent. Nevertheless, he was an avid baseball fan, and participated in the yearly Hollywood All-Stars games. Still, he longed to be able to get involved in a sport and, since tennis didn't seem too dangerous, he began to play often with Tom Mankiewicz that summer. Unfortunately, as with everything else, Bobby wanted to be an instant expert, and he was constantly frustrated by the fact that even if he played every hour of every day for a month, he still wouldn't be that good. As in show business, not only did he want to be good, he wanted people to see him as good. When he missed a ball, Mankiewicz would try to reassure him. "Yeah, well you're not so good," Bobby would growl defensively.

"Bobby was not the type of fellow to play bad tennis goodnaturedly," Tom remarked. Nevertheless, Tom didn't consider Bobby a bad sport. The fact that Darin would drive himself harder than anyone else even became "an oddly endearing quality."

Bobby was a devoted baseball fan and played in many of the Hollywood All-Stars games. Here he dresses for a game in 1966.

Chapter Twelve

*"If you don't try, if you don't do something
for yourself, you won't get anywhere."*
—BOBBY DARIN TO STUDENTS AT HIS ALMA MATER,
BRONX HIGH SCHOOL OF SCIENCE, 1967.

Bobby Darin was starting to realize that the world of show business was narrow and constricting. He knew he needed a cause to believe in, something that was larger than himself. In the presidential candidacy of Robert F. Kennedy, Bobby found what he was looking for. An article in *The New York Times* in February 1967, had piqued his interest. In it, RFK spoke of America's malaise of spirit and went on to strike a responsive chord in Bobby's own psyche, "As individuals we have far too little to say or do about these issues which have swallowed the very substance of our lives. We seek to recapture our country. That is what the 1968 election must really be about."

These were words and ideals Bobby strongly identified with. He'd always had a strong patriotic spirit, and he acutely felt the pain America was experiencing in the aftermath of the Watts riots. When Kennedy spoke of recapturing the country, Bobby grew excited. He wanted to be a part of the work, to feel that his own life could make a difference too.

In November 1967, Robert and Ethel Kennedy began organizing a telethon to benefit Washington's Junior Village Orphanage. Bobby was appearing at the Shady Grove Theater nearby and offered his services. He thoroughly enjoyed the day he spent at the orphanage. He found the children there full of the same hopes and aspirations he had had as a boy in the Bronx. Although he didn't feel qualified to give them specific advice, he did try to instill in them the confidence to make something of themselves. "If you don't try, if you don't do something for yourself, you won't get anywhere," he told them. "Sure, there are people out there in the world who can help you, but first you have to do something for yourself."

Later in the day, Bobby gave a concert, singing some of his own hits and such tunes as "Blowin' in the Wind." Then, sitting on a stool, with children all around him, he led a rousing rendition of "This Land Is Your Land."

With the new cause, Bobby also found a new love, columnist Barbara Howar. In addition to appearing on-camera during the telecast, Barbara had been asked to take charge of one of the celebrities. She was given the choice of Angie Dickinson or Bobby. She chose Bobby. Although he was seeing a number of other women, including singer Bobby Gentry, Bobby Darin and Barbara Howar now became an instant item.

Howar found Bobby surprisingly stimulating—and she found that traveling in his world could be unpredictable, to say the least. In Philadelphia, they talked race with Flip Wilson while eating at a hamburger joint; in Puerto Rico, the conversation was about censorship and their guest was Tony Franciosa. They started a brawl with a bar full of hookers in San Juan, and talked about the times with Sugar Ray Robinson, Gore Vidal, and Liza Minelli in Bobby's dressing room at the Copa.

Day in and day out, Bobby shouted at her to "open your eyes and look around," much in the same way he had with Sandy during their courtship in Italy. Barbara was, however, more willing to see than Sandy could ever be. Every day they spent together was an eyeopener. Later, she would recall: "He was a self-styled intellectual, a young man with a political conscience and the Elmer Gantry ability to convert those who did not share his convictions. I know it would make better reading to report that I began thinking of the world's problems through an exposure to John Kenneth Galbraith, but it was Mr. Darin who led me through the maze of bigotry in which I lived, backed me down on every narrow-minded point, and made me care. Whatever my Washington reputation suffered, Bobby Darin did fine things for my soul. At the very least, he showed me I might have one."

Politics excited Bobby more than show business ever had. As his social conscience grew, he began to think of running for office himself. Certainly, his new concerns affected his perception of his career. He told one reporter, "To be called the greatest entertainer may mean being paid more than anybody or having four limousines. Those are not essentials to me anymore. Being accepted universally as an entertainer and human being is." But just as Bobby was on the threshold of political self-awareness, events were set in progress that would lead to his psychological and spiritual destruction, events that had been thirty-one years in the making.

Early in 1968, the rumors of Bobby's political ambitions had reached their peak, and Nina was scared. She was sure that if Bobby ran for public office, somehow his opposition would discover the unsavory facts surrounding his birth and use this information to humiliate him. She discussed these fears with Vee, and they agreed that such a revelation could destroy him.

Nina's mind whirled in confusion. She knew that Bobby should be told the truth, yet Polly's warnings echoed through her mind. "Never, never tell him. He hasn't been raised in a way that would allow him to accept this." Nina fought with herself. And she prayed desperately that something would happen, that some event would take the burden from her shoulders so she wouldn't have to reveal her secret.

In mid-February, Bobby was appearing at the Latin Casino in Cherry Hill, New Jersey. On the day following his last performance, Nina and Vee came for a visit. During the two-hour drive, they discussed Nina's options, and by the time they had arrived at the Warwick Hotel in Philadelphia, where Bobby was staying, Nina had reluctantly accepted the inevitability of her confession.

"Bobby, is it true that you intend to go into politics?" she asked hesitantly, after the initial greetings were over.

"Yes," Bobby replied, "the Democratic Party of California is ready to sponsor me. All I have to do is find the right office to run for."

Nina realized that she could delay no longer.

Vee, also sensing that the time had come, went down to the lobby, leaving Nina and Bobby alone in his suite.

Again, Polly's words began haunting Nina, but she quickly put them out of her mind. Slowly, she turned to Bobby and said, "Sweetheart, you'd better sit down because there's something you must know."

Bobby's face was a study of confusion and apprehension. Something was seriously wrong, but what?

Nina took a good look at him. She remembered now the many times in the last thirty-one years when she'd wanted to call him son but had forced herself to call him brother instead. She remembered the endless days of caring for him when he was ill and her pride in the earliest achievements of his career. Still, she remembered her mother's warnings, "Don't tell him! Don't tell him!" *Polly was right,* Nina thought. *He'll never understand, but it's too late to turn back. He must know.* Looking directly into Bobby's eyes, Nina said the words she'd never thought she'd ever say, "I'm not your sister, I'm your mother."

A deadly silence came over the room. The seconds ticked away on her watch, the same watch he had inscribed years before, "To my favorite sister—Love, Dodd."

Bobby just stared at the woman in front of him.

"Oh my God, I should have known," he murmured hoarsely.

Images from the past rushed through his mind. He remembered an argument he'd once had with Nina when she had turned to him and said, "Don't you answer me like that again! No matter how old you get or how big you get, you'll never be too big for me to give you a good slap." Now these words came back, not as a sister's words, but as a mother's.

Conflicting emotions and questions welled up inside him. In his heart, Bobby knew that Nina was telling him the truth, but in so many ways he didn't want to believe it. Accepting what she had just told him meant accepting so much more, and in these first moments of shock he was not sure that he could handle all the repercussions. Nina's admission meant that his beloved Polly, who had preached honesty to him every day, had lied to him. And if Polly wasn't his mother, then Sam Cassotto wasn't his father. But if it wasn't Sam, then who could it have been?

"Who's my father?" he asked, dazed.

"I'm sorry, sweetheart, but that information will die with me. Your father never knew I was pregnant. The only person who knew who he was was Mama, and it's going to stay that way."

Suddenly, Bobby realized that the woman in front of him was a stranger. He had never really taken the time to get to know her, and now he wondered if it was too late. "You must be the strongest woman in the world. No, the strongest person in the world," he responded, staring through her.

Bobby stayed in his room for a long time after Nina and Vee had gone. His world had been turned upside down. There wasn't anything he could be sure of anymore, and so he grew unsure of himself. Until that afternoon, Bobby Darin had known exactly who he was and where he had come from. Now, with one powerful blow, Nina had inalterably shattered everything.

As time passed, Bobby grew bitter. Although these feelings were not consciously directed toward Polly, Bobby did nothing to hide the way he felt about Nina. He even found it hard to accept Nina's reasoning and her motivation in revealing her secret. He had expected his family to be perfect because they were *his* family. If Nina was overweight, or sometimes laughed a little too loud, or didn't dress as he would like her to, he somehow felt embarrassed. But he had never reckoned with her strength

A teenaged Bobby celebrating the holidays with family and friends. Bobby, in upper left corner;
Vee Walden below him; Charles Maffia, lower left; Rosie Duszik, standing in center;
Varina Cassotto, on the right in dark top; Polly Walden seated on the right; Vanna Maffia
bottom center; and Paula Duszik on bottom right.

of character, with the resolution that had been instilled in her by Polly. Bobby knew that Nina meant it when she told him his father's name would remain a secret. Although she didn't realize it at the time, her refusal to divulge his father's identity only caused further irreparable damage to her relationship with her son.

Later, when Bobby told Steve Blauner of Nina's refusal to discuss his father, Blauner somewhat naively assured him that the hospital records would have the information. But a check revealed that Nina had taken care of that possibility: on the birth certificate, the father's name had been left blank. When Charlie Maffia once foolishly suggested to Bobby that *he* could have been Bobby's father, Bobby snapped, "That's impossible, Charlie. My father had to have been intelligent. He had to be a doctor or a lawyer." Charlie was deeply wounded by Bobby's reaction; after all, he had grown to love Bobby as a son. Nevertheless, after Bobby's death, Charlie conveniently forgot that he had not met Nina until a year after Bobby's birth, and he began spreading the word that "Bobby Darin's sister was really his mother and I'm his father."

Over the remaining years in his life, Bobby would never successfully come to terms with the circumstances surrounding his birth. His feelings for Nina now were an obstacle. Nina had always been proud of her reputation for honesty and often had said, "You must remember, I never lie." Now, when such statements were made in Bobby's presence, he'd greet them with vehement derision; "You told the biggest lie a woman could ever tell. You denied your own child!"

Bobby's respect for himself and his own life had been shattered. "My entire life," he told Vee, "has been a lie."

Chapter Thirteen

*"I think I could do anything to you, and you'd
still love me."*

—BOBBY DARIN TO NINA CASSOTTO, 1968.

Bobby's personal heartache did little to cool his interest in politics or RFK's message of brotherhood. With characteristic zeal, Bobby carried his feelings into his stage act—with questionable results.

One night that spring, about two-thirds of the way through his show at the Copa, Bobby had the house lights turned up after his dramatic presentation of "Brother Can You Spare a Dime?" After delivering a sincere though somewhat lengthy speech about the American spirit and ideal, he said, "I'm very proud that there's a great American in my audience tonight, and I'd like you all to give him a warm reception." The audience grew restless as Bobby paused briefly before announcing, "Ladies and gentlemen, Dr. Martin Luther King."

Instead of an ovation, his announcement had been greeted by an ominous silence, and then the merest smattering of applause. It was an embarrassing moment for both Dr. King and Bobby, who realized for the first time that his growing political activism and his show business career might not always mix as comfortably as he had hoped.

When King was assassinated on April 4, Bobby was so shattered that he canceled his evening show at the Three Rivers Inn in Syracuse.

Bobby campaigned extensively for Robert F. Kennedy during his bid for the presidency in 1968. This shot was taken at a rally in Ohio.

Huddled by the radio, he listened attentively as Robert Kennedy encouraged an all-black crowd in Indianapolis to "replace that violence [and] bloodshed that has spread across our land with an effort to understand, with compassion and love." By this time, Robert F. Kennedy had already announced his candidacy for the presidency, and Bobby Darin had made up his mind to do all he could to help Kennedy's campaign. Late in May, Bobby flew to San Francisco with Kennedy's entourage to do some serious campaigning prior to the California primary, which was set for June 4. En route, the two men talked at length.

Kennedy appreciated the time Bobby was donating to his cause. In turn, Darin's admiration of Kennedy was rapidly becoming idolatry, and he was pleased that his idol could also be his friend. As they relaxed together on the plane, they sang songs—"Danny Boy" and "This Land Is Your Land" turned out to be mutual favorites—and Bobby even did the Bob Dylan classic, "Blowin' in the Wind." Afterwards, Robert Kennedy was heard to remark that only after hearing Bobby sing the song did he really appreciate Dylan's lyrics. As for Bobby, the trip had him convinced that he was right about Kennedy. "He was someone I could believe in," he declared.

Monday, June 3, Bobby joined Kennedy's final sweep through San Francisco's Chinatown. That evening, during his opening-night performance at Mr. D's, Bobby exhorted the audience to vote for Robert F. Kennedy, "the next president of the United States." The following day, Kennedy won the California primary. Bobby had watched the election coverage on television all day and had kept in close contact with Kennedy's headquarters. That evening, he watched as the television cameras panned out through the ballroom of the Ambassador Hotel in Los Angeles, showing the crowd as they sang "This Land Is Your Land" and chanted "We Want Kennedy!" Bobby desperately wanted to share his friend's moment of triumph; he'd made plans to fly down after his show to join in the postprimary celebration.

As Bobby Darin walked on stage at Mr. D's, the applause of his audience reminded him once again of the cheers for Kennedy at the Ambassador. He gave an inspired performance, his own celebration of Kennedy's victory. When he entered his dressing room after the closing number, the television was still on, but the crowd's ovation was drowning out the sound. Closing the dressing room door, Bobby took off his sweaty jacket—and stood still as the chilling words began to sink in. Kennedy had been shot; he was fighting for his life in a Los Angeles hospital. Darin exploded with rage, and within minutes he had destroyed all the furniture in his dressing room, smashing chairs and finally breaking the TV set. Then rage gave way to tears.

After canceling the remainder of his engagement, Bobby flew back to Los Angeles on the same flight he had expected to take to Kennedy's celebration. There he awaited further news of Kennedy's condition. Vee called from New York to be sure he was all right. Just the day before, they had had one of their most explosive debates about Kennedy, and now she regretted some of the things she had said. She told Bobby how sorry she was and asked him to call if he needed anything. "The country's in trouble," was all he could reply.

When he heard that Kennedy had died, Bobby called Barbara Howard and asked her to make arrangements for him to stay in Washington during the Kennedy services. Then he and his road manager, Marty Singer, flew to New York.

On the morning of June 8, Bobby was part of the crowd of mourners inside St. Patrick's Cathedral. He listened as Edward Kennedy paid moving tribute to his slain brother, and he cried unashamedly as the mourners sang "The Battle Hymn of the Republic." Then he and Marty Singer flew to Washington ahead of the Kennedy family and the silent, solemn funeral train.

Bobby arrived at the grave site ahead of the crowd and was immediately recognized by reporters, who asked him to make a statement. He refused, explaining that he wasn't there as a celebrity, but as a friend of Mr. Kennedy's. The press respected his wishes and left him alone.

The funeral train arrived in Washington late that afternoon, and as the casket was carried into Arlington National Cemetery it was followed by the Kennedy family and their friends. Behind them, thousands of mourners lit up the night with candles. Bobby stood on the edge of the crowd, not far from the Kennedy family, and listened as the prayers were said over the shroud. Tears streamed down his face.

Even after the services were over and the family had departed, Bobby felt compelled to remain with the multitudes holding a graveside vigil. Later, describing the experience, Bobby would say, "It was as though all my hostilities, anxieties, and conflicts were in one ball that was flying away into space, farther from me all the time, leaving me content with myself."

Through the early morning hours, as the crowds began to disperse and the workmen arrived to complete the grave, Bobby remained, a solitary observer watching the shadowy figures working in the dawn light. As the men lowered Kennedy's casket into the ground, Bobby felt as if they were burying a part of him too.

Bobby shows off his $100,000 handmade automobile, "The Bobby Darin Dream Car."

Soon Washington began to awaken to another day. For most, the dream that had become a nightmare was over; but for Bobby, the nightmare had just begun. From this time on, he would question and test all the codes that he had lived by, all the foundations of his life and his career.

Ever since his first success in 1958, Bobby had enjoyed the good life. He had adopted the style of a rich "movie star," and he and Sandy had developed the art of spending money to the point where it was almost a science. In the six years of their marriage, they had lived in a series of luxurious homes and had driven a collection of fabulous cars, including a $93,000 handmade dream car that was finished off with thirty coats of pearlized paint and showered with diamond dust.

Sandy would perfume herself only with "Joy," the most expensive scent on the market, and Bobby would go through flagons of "Zizanie." Shopping with either of them was an unforgettable experience. Bobby delighted in ordering "one of each in every color you've got" of anything he took a liking to. And with his kind of attitude, it's not surprising that he became quite a clothes horse. At one point, he owned sixty custom-made silk suits, over a hundred shirts, and fifty pairs of shoes.

Wherever the Darins went, there were people waiting on them hand and foot. Bobby maintained a large entourage on the road that usually included his valet (either Charlie Maffia or Andy DiDia), Sandy's hair-dresser, Dodd's nurse, Bobby's conductor, and often Bobby's manager. Once, when Bobby was going to Miami for an extended engagement at the Eden Roc, he rented a private Union Pacific Pullman car to transport Sandy, Dodd, and himself. Accompanying them on their trip were a cook, a private porter, Sandy's hairdresser, Dodd's nurse, and Bobby's manager, as well as a larder of caviar and a liberal store of chili.

After his divorcee, Bobby continued to live in the splendid surround-ings to which he had become accustomed. Between 1966 and 1968, he rented two magnificent homes in Beverly Hills and a townhouse in Manhattan. Each time he moved into a new home he would christen the kitchen with his favorite meal, Nina's manicotti, prepared by Nina her-self on the East Coast and then packed in dry ice and shipped to Bobby, wherever he might be.

Darin may have developed a lavish lifestyle, but he worked damned hard for his money—and he seldom took vacations. Every day he wrote and rehearsed, and practiced on any of half a dozen instruments. If he happened to be concentrating on a new composition, that song was all that was heard around the house for days. If a recording session was near, he would pore over the musical arrangements with his conductors for hours until he knew every note of every instrumentation inside out. The perfection apparent in Darin's work did not come easily, and he knew it.

After Kennedy's death, he questioned it all—the clothes, the lifestyle, and even the professional commitment. Bobby Darin had been carried away by a dream, by one man's vision of what was right and wrong with America. Now he desperately needed to contribute something meaning-ful to his world. And his work? Well, his work was just entertainment, and it no longer seemed important to the world around him. He ques-tioned whether anyone who had as little impact on people's lives as he had deserved to live as he did. There were contradictions inherent in his values, but he couldn't come to terms with them. He brooded for hours, for days, but the answers were elusive.

This inner turmoil affected the tenuous relationship he now had with his family. In the summer of 1968, Bobby rented a home on Malibu Beach for $5,000 a month and invited Nina and the kids out for the season. All but Vana came. It soon became apparent that Bobby still couldn't deal with his feelings about his family. Both Nina and Vee were vivacious, intelligent women who enjoyed a good laugh, even if it was on them. Bobby loved them dearly and enjoyed their company, especially Vee's. But somehow, somewhere, things just didn't feel right anymore.

He had traveled a long way since his boyhood in the Bronx. Sure, it was only three thousand miles on the map—but mentally he'd been to the moon and back. Yet Nina and Vee were unchanged. It was difficult now for Bobby to identify with the kid who had stolen bagels for breakfast. And sometimes his family was just too much of a reminder of the dire predictions that had been made in his childhood. Bobby found it hard to be in Nina's company for very long without remembering the days he had hovered near death as a child.

At times, he seemed to resent the fact that his family was always there for him. It made him feel guilty, especially when things were going well emotionally or professionally and he hadn't wanted them around to share it. His financial contributions to the Maffia household had continued in the same erratic pattern as before. He made a point of always paying for medical expenses, and he seldom turned down any specific requests for help. Nevertheless, he was not always there for his family when they needed him.

One day that summer, while Nina was in the kitchen, Bobby came in, opened the refrigerator, and took out a piece of fruit. Then he started to leave the room and, almost as an afterthought, paused in the doorway. "You know, Nina," he said, "I've been thinking. I think I could do anything to you and you'd still love me. Even if I was broke, I could still come home to you, couldn't I?"

Nina stopped what she was doing and looked up at him. For all his success and sophistication, he still seemed so vulnerable to her.

"Sweetheart, it's *you* we love, not your money. You didn't have any money when you were ten years old, and I took care of you. I'd do it all again, with all my heart, if I had to. You know you've always been special to all of us."

Nina could have used some of that kind of support from Bobby. She too was suffering through her own personal problems. The death of Polly, her closest confidante, had left an unfilled void. Although Nina had developed a close relationship with Vee, the two women were too much alike, and there was often friction between them. Vana had begun to build her own life and, while she remained close to her family, she somehow managed to remain aloof from their problems. Although Gary was already becoming an enormous comfort to Nina, he was still only a twelve-year-old child.

As for Charlie, he and Nina just didn't get along. Both had violent tempers, and while Charlie would unleash his verbally, Nina's reactions would tend to be more physical. It was not unusual for her to actually punch holes in the walls of their home—in fact, it became something of a private joke. When someone would enter the Maffia household and notice a hole in the wall, their immediate reaction would be, "Oh, Nina's been at it again!"

Charlie had been touring with Bobby off and on for about ten years, and Nina hadn't been at all upset by his absences, no matter how extended they might be. She discovered that whenever Charlie was expected home for a few days, her blood pressure went up. Before long, both Nina and Charlie's attentions were drawn elsewhere. When they were divorced, Nina legally resumed the use of her maiden name, and Charlie remarried.

By 1968, Nina was no longer a daughter or a wife or a sister—and Bobby wouldn't allow her to take on the role of a mother. She longed to hear him call her "Mother" just once. As each Mother's Day approached, she dreamt that Bobby might send her flowers, but he never did.

That summer, an idea started to germinate in Bobby's mind. He had to get away from all the pressures surrounding him so that he could think things out. It didn't seem possible to continue the kind of life he was leading. It wouldn't be easy: contracts had been signed and dozens of jobs hung in the balance. Nevertheless, that summer he began to narrow down his commitments.

On August 21, 1968, Bobby Darin sold Trinity Music to Commonwealth United Corporation for $1,300,000. Of this, Bobby received a flat one million dollars, with the rest going to his lawyer and to Ed Burton, Vice-President and General Manager of TM. Burton and the lawyers were paid in cash, but Bobby chose to take his money in CUC stock. CUC would purchase exclusive publishing rights to any music Bobby would write over the next five years. Unfortunately, a few months later CUC's stock dropped, and Bobby's million went down the drain.

Throughout the next year, Bobby continued the slow, careful liquidation of most of his holdings. He sold his various bits of real estate and started sorting out his possessions. Boxes were put into storage, and the rest of what he'd accumulated was given away to friends or charities. Finally, in June of 1969, he rented another home at Malibu Beach, this time for $10,000 a month. Again Nina, Vee, and Gary came out for the summer. Not long after they arrived, Bobby took Nina aside and told her, "There'll be no more money soon. I'm going away in the fall to think."

Many of those around him that summer tried to talk Bobby out of his plans, but Nina told them all patiently, "Don't worry about it. Ride it out. I've been through these things with him before. It's just a phase. It'll pass." Nina and the family left Malibu in early August. After they'd gone, Bobby continued to tie up more of his life's loose ends, visiting his friends to say goodbye.

Carol Lynley was one of Bobby's Malibu neighbors. One afternoon, she found him sitting on her porch playing the guitar. He was very depressed and seemed somehow preoccupied. He told her that he thought he would be dying in two years, and that he was going away for a while.

Another friend Bobby visited was Peggy Lee. As they sat quietly talking in her home, she felt the confusion that surrounded him. She felt powerless to help him, unable to give him any advice. He was so unhappy. She knew it would hurt him to give up his club work. Nevertheless, she told him, "If it will make you happy, do it—and good luck." She hoped he'd be all right, but there seemed to be so much inside that he couldn't verbalize.

The bitterness and confusion Bobby felt was evident to all of those around him. But he couldn't tell anyone about his feelings because he couldn't understand them either. He still hadn't come to terms with his own mortality and the contradictions it imposed on his public image. On stage, he was still the personification of self-assurance and masculine vitality; off stage, he wasn't even sure if he would be alive next week. The doctors had drawn the line for him at thirty. Now he was thirty-two and, as far as he was concerned, he was living on borrowed time.

It was only natural that the changes in Bobby's personal life would carry over into his records as well. During the eighteen months that he had been with Atlantic, he had had only two hits, "If I Were a Carpenter" and, to a lesser degree, "Mame." Nevertheless, during this period, he had released ten singles and five albums. Included in these was some of the finest work he had ever done. Two of the albums, *Dr. Doolittle* and *In a Broadway Bag,* would become Darin classics.

Bobby's rendition of "Feelin' Good" on the *Broadway* LP represents Darin at his best; his honky-tonk, brassy rendition of "Mame" was certainly the most joyous of the many recorded; and his gentle reading of "I'll Only Miss Her When I Think of Her," with its wry, bittersweet lyrical turns, showed his sensitive side. Finally, there is the soaring performance of "Night Song" from *Golden Boy.* In it, Bobby sings, "Hear it . . . life is in the air," and as he does so, the listener realizes that the key to Darin's excitement as a recording artist lies in that lyric. On this album, above all others, Darin comes across as a confident, intelligent performer at the peak of his talent and in full command of his material. A musical genius.

Bobby would probably have remained with Atlantic Records if he hadn't contemplated such drastic personal and professional changes. Major record companies tend to shy away from controversy and the lyrics that had begun to run through Bobby's head were somewhat out of the ordinary. With this in mind, he formed his own company, Direction Records, in September 1968.

It was a subdued Bobby Darin who explained to the press and public, "Events in the past eight months have affected me deeply, and it's only through my music that I can express myself. The purpose of Direction Records is to seek out statement-makers."

Ed Burton, now administrator of the new company, added, "For years, Bobby Darin has had a reputation as a finger snapper, but his first album on this label will establish a new image."

Bobby elaborated on Burton's news, "The album is solely comprised of compositions designed to reflect my thoughts on the turbulent aspects of modern society."

Bobby Darin Born Walden Robert Cassotto was released in late September, and it lived up to its advance publicity. The cover showed a nightclub photograph of Bobby Darin, clad in his tuxedo, superimposed over a photograph of Walden Robert Cassotto at the age of seven. Now Bobby saw himself as two different people.

With this album, the public was allowed to see the "other" Bobby Darin, to get past the image. The lyrical content conveyed a sense of Darin's return to his origins, without the material trappings he had acquired with his success. The songs were simple, but the stories they told were vivid. It was obvious to anyone who listened carefully that Bobby Darin was undergoing a period of intense self-examination and transition.

Each of the songs had been written by Bobby himself, and each made a strong statement. "In Memoriam," Bobby's musical reaction to the Kennedy assassination, told how "they never understood him, so they put him in the ground." "The Proper Gander" was a fable about the Vietnam War, and "Bullfrog" was an explanation of the history of our monetary system. Perhaps the most controversial, though, was "Long Line Rider," which told of the discovery of bodies at an Arkansas prison farm and the ineffectual inquest that followed.

In Memoriam

He's a ruthless opportunist
And he motivates by greed.
He's just the way his father was
And that we sure don't need.
So they all cried out destroy him
For he wants to see us drowned.
They never understood him
So they put him in the ground.

Now some had stood for hours
And some sat on the grass
Listening to their radios
For where the train had passed.
And a crowd will get impatient
As the clock hands turn around.
They never understood him
So they put him in the ground.

They handed out some candles
To the somber weary crowd
And told us not to light them
Till our eyes beheld the shroud.

Not even at that moment
Could there be tranquility
I could feel them push and argue
Hey, sit down, I cannot see.
They never understood him
So they put him in the ground.

When the fathers closed their bibles
And the family left the site,
The ropes and walls and hedges
Kind of faded in the night,
Replaced by all the people
Who made a prayerful sound.
They never understood him
So they put him in the ground.

Some people say the eighth of June
But the morning of the ninth
The workmen gently lowered him
By the beam of three work lights.
Easy, take it easy.
Set him down real slow.
He'd been on some rougher trips,
But he couldn't tell them so.
They never understood him
So they put him in the ground.

Now no man has the answers
And he was just a man.
And yet I can't help feelin'
That he knew a better plan,
A shorter road to justice

On the trip that's freedom bound.
But they never understood him
So they put him in the ground.

A second Darin album on Direction, entitled *Commitment,* followed soon after the first. There were more "message" songs, but they worked less well—except for "Song for a Dollar," an autobiographical sketch. In it, Bobby asks, rhetorically, "How many suits can you wear boy? And how many homes can you own?" Further on he sings, "For you flim-flam man, to get some fortune and fame." Although the album was not widely reviewed, those notices it did get were favorable.

Bobby's new kind of music needed new musicians. He had already lined up a young drummer, Tommy Amato, and a pianist, Bill Aikens, but just prior to recording the Direction material he had yet to find the right bass player. Then he was introduced to Quitman Dennis. He and Dennis got along well, both personally and musically. Dennis worked on both Direction albums and became one of Bobby's regular back-up men. Eventually, Bobby stood as best man at Jeanne and Quitman Dennis' wedding.

In Quitman Dennis, Bobby found a man in whom he could confide, a friend he could discuss his problems with. The PR men, agents, and managers were sticking it to him. They were eating him alive with percentages, feeding off him. He wasn't a greedy man, he confided to Dennis, but at this point he was already thinking about what he could leave Dodd, and the agents' percentages were eating into his son's legacy. "These parasites would send me to my grave to keep their own things going," was his bitter complaint.

Around this time, Bobby reorganized his nightclub act and brought it to the Coconut Grove and the Frontier. The program included some contemporary songs new to the Darin repertoire such as "Let the Good Times Roll" and "Dock of the Bay," as well as a particularly poignant rendition of the classic "Try a Little Tenderness." Also included were some of the less radical songs from the Direction LP. With this new program of material, Bobby moved even higher in stature as a nightclub entertainer. His material now had new and subtle shadings of drama. His nightclub act had become not only an exciting experience, but an emotional one.

With this new, more mature nightclub presentation, Bobby Darin made it clear that he did not intend to become a relic to be brought out at rock and roll revivals and fifties retrospectives. The "with it" finger-snapper had refined his image; he would not become some hideous anachronism. At the same time, Bobby made it equally clear that he was no longer willing to compromise his own ideals in order to meet the demands of others. This was made obvious in January of 1969, when he was scheduled to appear on a Jackie Gleason television show.

For the Gleason show, which was to be taped at the end of January and shown in April, Bobby had planned to sing two songs. One of these was "Long Line Rider," a choice approved by Peekskill Productions, producers of the show.

At 6:30 on the night of the taping, Bobby received a wire from CBS ordering him to delete a verse from "Long Line Rider":

> *That's the tale the warden tells*
> *As he counts his empty shells*
> *By the day, by the day.*
> *This kind of thing can't happen here*
> *'Specially not in an election year.*

Darin was flabbergasted. He'd sung the song on both ABC and NBC and on stage at the Copa with nary a complaint. Outraged that the network should try to censor his music, he walked off the show. Soon afterward, he brought a lawsuit against Gleason and CBS for $238,756 in damages, charging that CBS had acted at Gleason's direction and stating that it had been too late for him to substitute another song. When asked if he feared the repercussions from this unusual suit, Bobby firmly replied, "I don't care if I never do another TV show in my life."

Professionally there were no noticeable repercussions, but personally the incident made Bobby realize once and for all that political activism and show business made uneasy bedfellows. When he dug deeper into himself to understand just what was happening, instead of coming up with answers, he just seemed to come up with more questions.

From Florida and the Gleason Show, Bobby and his entourage flew directly to Mexico City, where he was to open a new nightclub, owned by the Castro Brothers. Opening night was a sensation, as usual, but Bobby's recent troubles had put him in a blue funk. He complained about everything—the acoustics, the local musicians, even the weather. After the second night, he announced that he had laryngitis and couldn't perform. As far as he was concerned, the engagement was over. The Castro Brothers had other ideas. When Bobby and his musicians attempted to turn their Mexican working papers in for their passports, the Mexican authorities refused. The only way Bobby could get back into the States was by hiding in an ambulance, crossing the border with sirens blaring and lights flashing.

Bobby's self-examination resulted in his recognition of a second identity, Bob Darin, the nonpublic personage behind the professional show-biz facade. Bob Darin was the man Walden Robert Cassotto had grown into, while Bobby Darin had become a character to be played on stage. What Bobby wanted to do was bring the two back together again.

At eight o'clock on the evening of July 23, 1969, Bob Darin appeared at the Bonanza Hotel Opera House in Las Vegas. The skin-tight black tuxedo was gone, replaced by a pair of jeans and a denim jacket. The toupee was gone as well, and his full orchestra was replaced by a quartet composed of Tommy Amato, Quitman Dennis, Bill Aitkins, and Bob Paythress.

His opening song, "Gabriel," was a rock number that had previously been recorded by Joe South. Other songs in his act that night included "Lady Madonna," "Lonesome Whistle," and Dylan's "I'll Be Your Baby

Tonight." Bob Darin rocked through his new repertoire as if he had been doing it for years. When one fan called out for "Artificial Flowers," he responded, "That was yesterday," and then went on with his planned program. Finally, Bob Darin picked up his own well-worn guitar and sang his latest composition, "Simple Song of Freedom."

Standing alone on stage, in full command of the crowd before him, he sang the refrain, over and over, "Let it fill the air, tell the people everywhere, we the people here don't want a war." It was the most powerful song he had ever written, and the audience responded enthusiastically. Their applause swept over him in waves, easing any pain that might have been caused by his exhausting performance. From that night on, "Freedom" would remain the one moment in every show when Bobby felt everything come together for him.

Simple Song of Freedom

CHORUS:
Come and sing a simple song of freedom,
Sing it like you've never sung before.
Let it fill the air, tell the people everywhere,
We the people here don't want a war.
Hey there Mr. Black Man can you hear me?
I don't want your diamonds or your game,
I just want to be someone known to you as me
And I will bet my life you want the same.

(chorus)

Seven hundred million are you listening?
Most of what you read is made of lies,
But speaking one to one, ain't it everybody's sun
To wake to in the mornings when we rise?

(chorus)

Brother Solzhenitsyn are you busy?
If not, won't you drop this friend a line?
Tell me if the man who is plowing up your land
Has got the war machine upon his mind.

(chorus)

No doubt some folks enjoy doing battle
Like presidents, prime ministers, or kings.
So let us build them shelves
Where they can fight it out among themselves,
And leave the people be who love to sing.

(chorus)

♪

Chapter Fourteen

"I've been running a long time and it's taken a lot out of me—mentally and physically. Now, I just want to do my own thing."
—Bobby Darin to Dick Clark, 1968.

There are many people who feel that Big Sur is the most beautiful place in America. The town itself is an inconspicuous Pacific shore community about a hundred and fifty miles south of San Francisco where the Big Sur River meets the sea. But over the years, the name Big Sur has come to stand for the entire fifty-mile stretch of spectacular coastline just below Carmel.

To men used to the concrete jungles of Manhattan and the plastic facades of Beverly Hills, the rocks, ocean, and sky at Big Sur seem like Nirvana. More than just real estate, Big Sur is a state of mind. For years, writers, artists, and photographers—from Jack London and Henry Miller to Ansel Adams—had found in Big Sur's relentless exposure to the energy of nature the perfect atmosphere for their own creative energies. Bobby was no different. It was to this paradise that he fled in the early autumn of 1969. He rented a piece of farmland from a man by the name of Jan Brewer in an area known as Fifer's Beach. Then he bought a fourteen-foot house trailer, and went into total seclusion. He traded the silks and custom tailoring for a half a dozen pairs of jeans.

Shortly after arriving, he wrote to Nina: "I am now a turtle. Virtually everything I own is on my back and suffice it to say I am one ton lighter and therefore 2,000 pounds happier. All houses are gone. All extraneous (everything except LPs, tapes, books and personal doodads) items have been sold and I am out from under. I wish all of you the serenity of this area and the peace of these mountains."

He spent his time chopping wood, reading, and even digging his own sewage system. For relaxation, he would just listen to his tapes or work on his music. Most of all, he tried to relax his mind so that he could think clearly about the seemingly endless pressures of his life, pressures that were making him feel as if things were closing in on him. Usually, his only company were the hundreds of monarch butterflies that inhabited the area, giving it the appearance of a fairyland.

Bobby used Big Sur the way others use a psychiatrist's couch. He gave up his body and his mind to the earth's beauty, relaxing as he never had before. He was cleansing both his mind and his soul. "I've confessed to the breeze. . . ." wrote Vincent Youmans, and Bobby did basically the same. Wandering through the glory of the land, he felt as one with the majesty around him. He saw things more clearly than he ever had before.

Living as anonymously as possible, he melted into the sparsely populated area. One of the few couples Bobby did come in contact with were Mr. and Mrs. Walter Trotter, natives of the area who really didn't know "what a Bobby Darin was." They had been told by some of the more worldly locals that the guy in the trailer was a celebrated singer, but they were unimpressed. If Trotter was working, and Bobby happened to be in the area, Bobby would sometimes pitch in. If he didn't, Trotter was likely to comment, "You lazy son of a bitch, help out or get lost!"

One day, Bobby was sitting in the doorway of his trailer strumming his guitar when Trotter happened by. Turning toward him, Trotter drawled, "I hear you can play that damn thing, and I guess you might even be able to sing." Bobby looked up and, suppressing a laugh, responded, "Yeah, well, I have been known to do that from time to time."

While in Big Sur, Bobby gave his imagination free reign. No problem was too large for his consideration. He looked for solutions to starvation in India and political problems in Africa, the erosion of relics in Rome, and the threat of communism. Often during this period, he would call Tom Mankiewicz to discuss his newest idea, and the two men would analyze it from every direction possible.

These calls to Tom Mankiewicz were among the few contacts Bobby had with the outside world. During his first few months at Big Sur, he seldom left the area. Many days were spent in the library at Carmel reading everything from Nietzsche to Dickens. At the trailer, he would relax by listening to Mozart or Tchaikovsky. Evenings were spent looking out over the coastline, watching as the changing light played games with the water and the rocks. Few letters were written; the one to Nina was the only one she received, although periodically Bobby would call just to let her know that he was all right. Most of Bobby's friends didn't hear from him for months at a time, and he had absolutely no contact with the press.

True to form, with no real news to report, rumors began to build—not in any of the major media but in the underground rock press and the grocery-store scandal sheets. They spoke of acid trips and orgies and insinuated that Bobby Darin had gone off the deep end. He had turned into a freaked-out hippy, undergoing one psychedelic experience after another.

But none of it was true. Bobby had seen through Polly's experience to the dark side of drug addiction, and, through showbiz people around him, the horrors of alcoholism. He wanted no part of these, or any other weaknesses. The shadow of death, which so relentlessly pursued him, was enough of a monkey on his back. Throughout his adult lifetime, Bobby spoke out strongly against alcohol and drugs. Although at one point he told a friend that he and Bobby Kennedy had smoked pot and sung peace songs together, most of the time Bobby would drink nothing but beer or wine, and he seemed deeply suspicious about the use of any kind of drugs.

If it's true that Bobby's mind went through new experiences during this time, then they were brought about by the sheer exhilaration he felt at cutting the ties that had bound him and putting himself in nature's hands. Bobby managed to keep his life at Big Sur intensely private—it would forever remain a secret between himself and the rocks and the sea.

Before leaving for Big Sur, Bobby was offered a small but important role in a film entitled *The Happy Ending,* written, directed and produced by Richard Brooks (who had written such films as *Elmer Gantry, Sweet Bird of Youth,* and *The Last Time I Saw Paris,* and would later produce and direct *Looking for Mr. Goodbar*). Brooks was married to the beautiful and talented British actress Jean Simmons, who would star in the film. For years, Bobby had had a crush on Miss Simmons, and he jumped at the opportunity to work with her.

Bobby's role was that of an Italian gigolo with whom Miss Simmons' character has a brief affair, only to discover that he is really an American. It was a rather sensuous role for Bobby, and although he had no particularly strong dramatic scenes, he came across very well. Darin's character's appeaance in the film mirrored his own look in 1968, with his short neat toupee and trim moustache.

No other film offers followed, so once Bobby had settled down into his new routine at Big Sur, he began to develop his own film project. The idea for a screenplay had been growing in his mind for a while, and it was during this period that he finally put it down on paper. Called *The Vendors,* it was a seamy look at a prostitute with a heart of gold who falls in love with a drug addict. The idea was old hat, and Bobby added no new insights.

While working on the screenplay, he showed it to a few of his friends, but none of them were very impressed. Dick Clark, for one, told him it was "dreadful." Interestingly enough, Bobby never showed the script to two of his closest friends, Tom Mankiewicz and Peter Stone, both top screenwriters. Most likely, he had convinced himself that he could dismiss the negative reactions of others, but he wouldn't be able to ignore similar verdicts from Mankiewicz or Stone.

Bobby had to finance the production himself, and also took on the jobs of producer and director. This work gradually brought him out of his isolation. By the early part of 1970, he was ready to begin filming. In the lead roles, he cast his old friend Richard Bakalayan (they had appeared in *Pressure Point* together), Gary Wood, Dick Lord, and Mariette Hartley.

Although Bobby was exciting to work with, the actors often found him a frustrating director. None of them ever saw an entire script; instead, each actor was given only those pages on which his or her lines appeared. Bobby had a very definite idea about what he wanted from this film, and he worked his actors mercilessly until they responded in the manner he wanted. At the same time, he earned their respect—it was obvious that he wasn't asking them to work any harder than he was himself.

As it turned out, none of the stars of the film—and virtually no one else—ever saw the film. Bobby spent months, years, editing and scoring it; but even as a completed film, it just wasn't very good. The $350,000 Bobby had spent in production costs would have to be chalked up to therapy.

While living in Big Sur and working on *The Vendors,* Bobby made sporadic visits to Las Vegas and Los Angeles to settle business matters or fulfill previous commitments. One of the latter took place in December 1969, when Bobby made a short return trip to Las Vegas for a two-week engagement at the Sahara, at the rate of $40,000 a week. As if to advertise his new image, Bobby had a life-size figure of "Bob Darin," dressed in a Levi suit and cowboy hat, placed in front of the entrance to the Sahara's Congo Room.

The Sahara engagement was an unmitigated disaster. The mink-draped, diamond-bedecked audience simply was not interested in denim and peace songs. They wanted the suave Bobby Darin they were familiar with, not this stranger singing songs about dead convicts and Alexander Solzhenitsyn. This was the first time that one of Bobby's nightclub audiences had responded negatively, and throughout the engagement the audiences' reactions were the same. They would listen to the first few songs, selected from Bobby's Direction albums, and then they'd begin to walk out. Bobby was horrified; once the audience began leaving, there was nothing he could do to get them back. Of course, he could always try returning to his old repertoire, but he refused to compromise. When the two weeks were up, he returned to Big Sur, more confused than ever.

Throughout his stay at Big Sur, Bobby maintained an office in Hollywood. It was located in the same building as Dick Clark's offices. Whenever he was there, seeing to the production of *The Vendors,* Bobby would stop in to see his old friend. Clark, of course, was aware of the identity crisis that Bobby was undergoing. Darin had helped Clark through some serious crises of his own, and now Dick hoped that he could help Bobby. During one of Bobby's visits, the conversation grew serious. "You're a latter-day hippie," Clark scolded.

Bobby argued back, telling Dick that this was no false front—this finally was the real Bob Darin. "Believe me, Richard," Bobby pleaded, "that other guy just wasn't me." The super showbiz character he'd been playing for years was dead and gone.

Dick Clark knew better. Such identity crises weren't unusual with entertainers; Bobby's was just lasting longer. Dick grew impatient, but he stopped himself from actually chastising his friend. Nevertheless, he told Bobby, "Go back and put on the tuxedo and go to work. Do what the people expect of you. They don't want to see a balding hippie sitting on a stage in Las Vegas."

Bobby shook his head. "I've been running a long time, and it's taken a lot out of me—mentally and physically," he answered quietly. "Now I just want to do my own thing."

Common sense told Bobby that much of what Clark said was true, but still he was having trouble sorting it all out. As Bobby left Clark's office, Dick couldn't help but feel that his friend looked like a lost soul. It's possible that Dick Clark's advice wasn't wasted. Later that month, when the Landmark Hotel in Las Vegas asked Bobby to appear, he was ready to leave Big Sur and give Vegas another shot. The disaster at the Sahara, his work on *The Vendors,* and the concern shown for him by his friends had all come together—he needed to step back a bit and look at his new life from a different perspective. He realized that he could do his peace songs and still do "Mack the Knife" too, that each had their appropriate place in his work. He realized that retirement was not the only way to resolve his inner conflicts. By shutting people out, he had only hurt himself more. He hadn't been enjoying his nightclub work the way he used to, he'd been finding it hard to face audiences—so why should he be surprised that they couldn't face him? But now Bobby was excited by the prospects the future held. He looked forward to getting back to work.

In preparing his new program, Bobby struck a compromise he could live with. This time, there were only half a dozen peace songs, and the more obscure ones, such as "Long Line Rider," were prefaced by simple explanations. The rest of the program was filled in with some contemporary songs and a few of Bobby's most popular hits. This mix worked out very well, and a two-week, open-ended engagement was expanded to six weeks.

After this stint, Bobby rapidly reemerged into Hollywood society. He and Shirley Jones had been close friends for some time, brought together by a mutual professional admiration and the fact that their children went to school together. They met once in a while for lunch or dinner. During one such meeting after Bobby's return from Big Sur, he told her, "I've done a lot of things and I've been a lot of people, but now I've come to realize who I am."

Throughout the next few months, Bobby's career began to build momentum. He seemed at peace with himself, and his work was getting the sort of sensational reviews he had always been used to. His old friends were glad that he was back, and were eager to see him again.

In October of 1970, Harriet Wasser flew to Toronto to visit with Bobby while he was filming a Canadian TV special called "The Bobby Darin Invasion." But when she walked into the studio where Bobby was working, Harriet sensed immediately that something was wrong.

The set was very quiet and Bobby, sitting on the floor in the corner, looked very ill. As she walked up to him, she heard another man telling him, "Don't worry, Bob. Take it easy, rest awhile. You'll feel better."

Harriet knelt by Bobby's side. As she did so, she noticed that his complexion was pasty and he was shivering. Her fear mounting, she asked, "Bobby, what's wrong? What's wrong?"

For a moment, Bobby couldn't even look at her. Then, with tears in his eyes, he said, "Hesh, I've been sitting here for half an hour, doing nothing, and my heart feels as if I've been running a marathon."

Years before, Polly had told Harriet about the seriousness of Bobby's condition, and she realized that he could be in very real danger now. She didn't know what to do. A doctor was en route, he told her, and then added weakly, "Hesh, I'm scared. I'm real scared." He began to cry.

Harriet put her arms out and held him, realizing as she did how old and frail he seemed.

"No one must know, Hesh," Bobby pleaded. "If my family hears about this, I'll know where they found out."

—♪—

Chapter Fifteen

"This isn't just a hobby. It's not fun and games. It's my life, and I want it to be right."
—BOBBY DARIN DISCUSSING SHOW BUSINESS IN 1970.

The doctors called it "fibrillations of the heart," and he'd been having them for hours at a time. His heart would beat 140 to 160 times a minute instead of the normal 60 to 80. This wasn't new to Bobby, but now the attacks had become more frequent and he was getting scared. Often he would have to enter the hospital for two or three days so that the doctors could stop and then restart his heartbeat at the right rhythm.

Surgery was the only solution. The specialists said that at least two of his four heart valves were malfunctioning and had to be replaced. There was no putting it off. Bobby considered all of this carefully. It was no surprise to him. For years, he'd known that some sort of surgery would be necessary. He was 34, four years older than he'd ever expected to be. So what did he have to lose?

He had already been booked for a four-week engagement at the Desert Inn in Vegas. The run would begin on January 10, and he was determined to see it through. No one realized then that Bobby didn't expect to live through the operation. And even if he did, he thought he'd never be able to perform again. He pleaded for one last chance to hear the roar of the crowds, for one more success to end his career. "You give me these six weeks to work, the first six weeks in 1971," he told his doctors. "Somehow, you keep me alive by remote control, and the moment I close, I'll go home, spend four hours with my son, and then I'll check into the hospital and give myself to you."

Getting Bobby through the four-week engagement at the Desert Inn was far from easy. He was very weak, and his energy level was almost nil. Besides, all this emotional pressure was having an effect on his heart. On stage, he was working harder than ever before. His performances crackled with the energy and vitality that his audiences had grown to expect. Off stage, he paid brutally for every minute.

He spent hours in bed. Shortly before the first show, he would get dressed and head down to his dressing room to await his cue. While performing, he'd sneak gulps of oxygen between numbers to bolster his draining energy. After his first show, he'd eat a bowl of spinach and a large steak and then do another performance. Afterwards, he'd retire to bed and stay there until the next night's show. This went on for twenty-eight days with no breaks.

During the engagement, Bobby always kept a stethoscope with him. Often he'd ask Bob Rozario, his conductor, to listen to his heartbeat. To Rozario, it sounded like "someone playing the drums very badly."

After the second show on the final evening, Bobby tearfully said his goodbyes and got into the back of his blue van. The ordeal he'd just been through almost made him look forward to a stay in the hospital. At the end of the all-night drive to Los Angeles, he saw Dodd, his nine-year-old son. Words eluded him. He knew that Dodd couldn't understand. Instead, Bobby hugged the boy closely. "Wherever I am, you know I love you," he said.

"Don't worry, Dad," replied Dodd, "everything's going to be fine."

After Dodd left, Bobby called Nina. He wanted to say goodbye, but he didn't want to tell her about his impending surgery. He knew the news would upset her, that she'd insist on being with him, which was the last thing he needed. No, he wanted to struggle and die on his own. He told Nina he was going on a vacation, a sea voyage. He'd be unavailable for six weeks, but he'd call if and when he made port. The story seemed to work.

The nine-hour operation was a success, but Bobby's attempt to keep it private was a failure. The next day, Vee Vee heard a news flash on the radio and informed Nina. After two days of frantic phone calls, she finally reached Bobby's doctor, Marvin Levy. Patients in intensive care, he told her, aren't allowed visitors; it would be best to stay where she was and wait for news.

Bobby remained in intensive care for five days. During that time—and even after, when he was moved to a private room—Bobby's heart almost stopped four times. Steve Blauner and his wife witnessed one of these attacks. Before the doctors came, Steve's wife kissed Bobby's hand, a farewell gesture that terrified him. "Don't let me die! Oh God, I'm going to die," he screamed as the Blauners were hurried from the room. Outside, Blauner turned to his wife and said, "I'm never going to see him again."

But Bobby was stronger than anyone thought, and he pulled through. In May of that year, he celebrated his thirty-fifth birthday—and with good cause. There was a new woman in his life, a beautiful young divorcee named Andrea Yaeger, whom he'd met in his lawyer's office. Although she had been upset by his operation and had left town, she was home now, with her two children, ready to nurse Bobby back to health.

There was another good reason to celebrate this particular birthday. Thirty-five was the outside limit Bobby's first doctor had put on his patient's survival. As difficult as the game had been, he seemed to have beaten the odds—at least temporarily. Bobby's doctors had already explained that artificial valves were seldom permanent and that eventually he would probably need another operation. Furthermore, they cautioned, his chances of surviving a second operation were just three to one. "But," he quipped to Tom Mankiewicz, "the odds are a hundred percent that I'll die if I don't have it."

He hid his feelings fairly well at the party he threw for the doctors

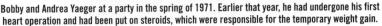

Bobby and Andrea Yaeger at a party in the spring of 1971. Earlier that year, he had undergone his first heart operation and had been put on steroids, which were responsible for the temporary weight gain.

and nurses from Cedars of Lebanon Hospital. For the combination birthday/survival celebration he'd turned his back yard into a carnival, complete with tents and tarot card readers. Caterers wandered the grounds with tray after tray of food while other vendors dispensed hot dogs, hamburgers, cotton candy, and popcorn. With Andrea at his side, he mingled with his friends and doctors. Eventually, he was so overwhelmed by the outpourings of love that he broke down and cried. Tom Mankiewicz sensed the bittersweet pain behind those tears. "Even by doing the only thing he could," Mankiewicz observed, "there was still a chance that he might not live much longer."

Bobby rested until the end of July. After the operation, he had been put on steroids, which caused him to gain weight. He grew a red beard and stopped wearing his toupee. Friends who'd been unaware of his health problems were shocked by his appearance. But Bobby was happy just to be alive. "Everybody, sooner or later, will have to go under the knife. Let's hope they make out as well as I did," he told the press.

As his strength returned, Bobby took on some television work. In January of 1972, he made appearances on *Cades County* and *Ironsides*, as well as a few Flip Wilson shows. In one very weird segment of Rod Serling's *Night Gallery* series, Bobby even ended up as a can of dog food!

Soon Bobby was also strong enough to perform again. In February 1972, one year after the operation, he opened at the Copa. Not only was he sensational, but he was the old Bobby Darin, the Bobby Darin that audiences all over the world had been applauding for sixteen years. No less than *The New York Times* noted, "Darin is still a first-class performer. He sang, played the guitar, drums, and piano, and managed to pull a lackadaisical first-night audience out of its lethargy."

Both physically and mentally, Bobby was feeling much better. Above all, he was grateful for what he considered "a little extra time." "I've got a love affair with this business, and the more you love something, the more you want to make sure everything goes right. This isn't just a hobby. It's not fun and games. It's my life, and I want it to be right."

He'd also come to terms with the different facets of his personality. "I realized that I need to be anonymous on the street and somebody else on the stage," he explained. "I had tried to put my street self on the stage, but then I began to look at myself and think, 'No, that's not it!' What they want is an actor on stage. An actor wears a costume and make-up. I'm an actor. There's nothing wrong with that. You go out and entertain them. If what they hear is what they see, then let me put on my tux. I'm comfortable in it. I don't have any inner arguments anymore."

That spring, the new/old Bobby Darin made numerous nightclub and television appearances. Bobby Darin Music was formed and, after considerable negotiations with Commonwealth United, Bobby got the copyrights back for all the songs he had written since the sale of Trinity Music. Following the release and failure of his second Direction album, he signed with Motown and recorded his Desert Inn act as his first album for the new label. Early that summer, NBC announced that *The Bobby Darin Amusement Company* would appear as a summer replacement for *The Dean Martin Show*. Bobby was coming back strong now.

Dean Martin Presents The Bobby Darin Amusement Company premiered on NBC on July 10, 1972, at 10 o'clock. It was obvious that the program had been planned to show off Darin's versatility. Each show opened with Bobby's Groucho Marx impersonation, then he'd sing a song and chat with the audience. The remainder of the hour moved back and forth between Bobby's songs, songs by his guest stars, duets with his guests, and comedy routines involving any one of Bobby's varied characters—including Dusty John Dustin, the poet laureate of the road; Angie, a boy from the Bronx; and the Godmother, a character who looked a bit like Marlon Brando in drag.

Bobby wasn't always easy to work with. In fact, his producers, Saul Ilson and Ernest Chambers, found that it was very hard for him to trust anyone. But at the same time Bobby desperately wanted the show to be a success and, once he came to know Ilson better, their relationship settled down. Still, there were times when Bobby's renewed self-assurance grew somewhat shaky. During one of these, he told Ilson, "You know, it's a hard thing to get up in the morning and have to become Bobby Darin. Bob Darin is a no one, but in the morning, as he looks in the mirror, he kind of grows in stature. Then, he puts on his rug and, all of a sudden, I'm Bobby Darin."

Throughout the series' production, Bobby tried to control his work schedule so that it would not affect his health. Each show would take four days of rehearsal and taping. Following this, Bobby and Andrea would hop in his car and take off for the Big Bear Mountains, east of

Bobby recording at Motown, circa 1972. Jimmy Haskell was the arranger and the studio was filled with the best musicians in Los Angeles.

Los Angeles. There they would camp out, cooking their own meals and resting until it was time to do the next show, three days later.

When the summer season was over and industry scuttlebutt rumored a fall series, Motown released *Bobby Darin*. In this album, Bobby's voice sounded considerably more mature and lived-in, earthy, bitter, worldly, strained, and yet utterly natural.

Late that summer, Bobby flew to Nova Scotia to work in a film entitled *Happy Mother's Day, Love George* with Patricia Neal, Cloris Leachman, and Ron Howard. After completing the film, Bobby went to Philadelphia for an appearance at the Latin Casino. While there, he happened to wander into a bookstore to do some browsing and discovered a fellow chess player in the owner of the store, a young man by the name of Larry Teacher. Over the next few days, the men became good friends, and since Bobby and Andrea were planning a vacation in Barbados in October, Bobby asked Larry and his wife Marilynn to join them.

When Bobby and Andrea arrived in Barbados they were greeted by a limousine driver who claimed to be the biggest Bobby Darin fan in the country. When Bobby expressed disbelief, the man swore that he had every Bobby Darin album ever made in the trunk of his limousine. Still doubtful, Bobby assured the driver that if what he said was true, he could be their driver for their entire Barbados stay. At this, the trunk was opened—and Bobby had himself a permanent driver.

Larry and Marilynn Teacher arrived a few days later and settled into the huge home Bobby had rented for their stay. Bobby had insisted that the house have a grand piano, but he never touched it during the time the Teachers were there. This was not the only sign that Bobby might not be completely his old self. There was at least one occasion when Bobby did not feel well and stayed in his room for the entire day.

Perhaps Bobby was becoming aware that his second operation would soon be needed. At least he had begun to brood about the future—and that of his son. That fall, Bobby had a weekend engagement at the Concord in the Catskills, and he took Dodd along with him. Dodd's trips to the East Coast had been few, and Bobby took this opportunity to show his son all his old stamping grounds. The Bronx of his youth was a burned-out ruin, but Bobby didn't seem to notice. As they drove through the city streets he told Dodd simply, "This is where I lived."

Vee Vee and Gary had recently bought some land in the Catskills, and along with Nina were living there in a house trailer nestled by a freshwater creek. Bobby and Dodd spent the next day there, enjoying Nina's cooking and relaxing by the water. It was the first time in years that the whole family had been together. It would also be the last.

Bobby traveled back and forth between New York and California quite a few times that fall, to another engagement at the Concord and a ten-

Darin returned to New York in January 1973 to record what would be his last release,
"Happy." Gravely ill, he paused for a picture with Harriet Wasser.

day run at the Copa. In between, he worked with Bob Crewe for
Motown and recorded the theme from the film *Lady Sings the Blues,*
entitled "Happy." Throughout the session, he suffered severe heart pal-
pitations, which left him pale and shaking. The inner pressure was
mounting daily. Nevertheless, he called upon whatever inner strength he
had and gave a superb reading of the lyrics. Bobby's recording of

"Happy," which would be his last, was to stand as one of the most powerful and dramatic recordings of his career.

Now there was no longer any time for rest. Upon returning to the West Coast, Bobby learned that NBC had picked up his series option and wanted it on the air on January 19. Production had to commence immediately.

The shows were beautifully done and critically acclaimed, but it was obvious they were draining him. When Bobby appeared during the closing number of each show, he was sweating profusely and looked exhausted. Even though the fibrillations were coming more and more often, Bobby was always the first one at rehearsals and the last one to leave. When the day's work was done, he went directly home, ate a simple dinner and crashed. After disconnecting the telephone, Andrea would sit by his bedroom door, just in case there was an emergency.

As Bobby's health deteriorated, he became argumentative and hard to please. For the first time, he began to feel uncomfortable with his audiences. He didn't seem to be focusing on them; there was no rapport. Perhaps he needed contact lenses, the producers suggested. "I don't want to be able to see the audience," was his reply.

During the taping of the final four shows, Bobby was emotionally and physically ragged. He was angry because he felt that no one understood what he was going through. To those around him, including Saul Ilson, his executive producer, he appeared to be sinking. Often, he'd be so depressed that he wouldn't feel like performing at all—and when the time came for him to do the audience warm-up, he would resist. Ilson would be forced to beg and cajole, but in the end, once Bobby was out there, hearing the audience's applause, he'd be revived.

By the time the final show rolled around, Bobby was at the emotional bottom. His impatience and intolerance with the crew over the past few weeks had brought them to an impasse. Ilson was constantly at Bobby's side, trying to prop him up. The plans called for Bobby to perform a large segment of his club act, with Peggy Lee doing a guest set. It would be a tough day's shooting. When Bobby heard that there wasn't enough time for a rehearsal, he became hysterical. "How could you do this to me?" he screamed at Ilson.

Ilson tried to calm Bobby down. Four cameras would be shooting, and there was no reason for Bobby to be worried. They managed to begin the taping, but soon Bobby started making remarks about his crew's performance. The camera work wasn't up to par and the audio was lousy, he complained. By the time the four o'clock union break rolled around, there was only one number left to be shot. Normally, this would have been no problem. If the crew was polled and a majority agreed to waive the break, the taping could continue. When the crew voted for a break, Bobby was stunned. He couldn't believe that he had so alienated these men that they would intentionally hurt him. As the crew cleared the set, Bobby slowly lowered himself to the floor, a very lonely man.

Despite the fact that his two-week engagement at the Las Vegas Hilton that April had been a huge success, Bobby started to become obsessed with his finances. His medical treatments were depleting his savings. Fearing that the end was near, he often spoke of wanting to put away enough for Dodd's future. Frantic for one last big score, he contacted Steve Blauner, the manager he'd let go when he'd left club work years before.

Since those good old, bad old days, Steve Blauner had become quite successful working for Columbia Screen Gems. Financially, he didn't need Bobby, and he didn't need the aggravation of dealing with his traumas. But Blauner had never gotten the Darin drug out of his system, and he couldn't say no. His only out would be to concoct a deal so outrageously unreasonable that *Bobby* would have to say no. They met for lunch at Lynnie's Restaurant in Beverly Hills, and Blauner laid his terms on Bobby. He demanded a one million dollar guarantee against 20 percent over five years; he would not travel with Bobby and would not work on weekends; Darin could not interrupt him during meetings and could not phone him after six in the evening.

Regretfully, Blauner explained, "Bobby, you're just not number one with me anymore—you can't be. I'm married now, and my family has to come first." Then he admitted, "You'd be a fool to sign this contract."

Blauner's plot failed miserably. Whether through desperation or fear of losing his grip on reality, Bobby signed the contract. Of course, he still interrupted Blauner in meetings and still called him after six, but now he apologized when he did.

Darin's salary in Vegas had always been one of the highest in the business—only Sinatra made more. But in March Blauner went Sinatra one better by negotiating a three-year, two million dollar, twenty-seven week deal with the MGM Grand Hotel. It worked out to an unprecedented $74,000 a week. Blauner also booked Bobby for a three-month spring and summer tour. The itinerary included concerts in Mt. Airy, Pennsylvania; Buffalo, New York; Cleveland, Ohio; Wallingford, Connecticut; Warwick, Rhode Island; Indianapolis, Indiana; Kansas City, Missouri; Pueblo, Colorado; and Los Angeles, California. There was also to be a one-week stint at the Latin Casino. All in all, it would have amounted to over sixty shows in a period of three months. Bobby knew that such a schedule would kill him. The tour would have to be cancelled. Blauner was left high and dry. Although both men knew that this was the only way out, the cancellation of the tour added further strain to a relationship that was reaching the breaking point.

Shortly afterward, Blauner and his wife were having dinner at home with some friends when Bobby turned up. His appearance was ghostly, and even Blauner's young daughter, who had always adored Bobby, noticed it. Frightened, she tried to hide in her father's lap. Blauner realized that there was something on Bobby's mind, and before long he got to it.

"About our relationship," Bobby told him, "both professionally and personally, it's a wrap."

Blauner tried to keep the conversation light, but he was having trouble holding his emotions in check. He asked his friend, "If you're walking down the street and I see you, should I turn around to avoid you?"

Bobby just shrugged.

"Bobby," Steve continued, "I'll always love you. You do what you have to do." After Bobby left, Blauner and his guests agreed that Bobby Darin looked like a beaten man.

Two weeks later, Bobby called Blauner and told him that he wanted to see him. When the two men got together, they embraced and Bobby apologized for the bad scene at Blauner's home.

Sickness was now steadily draining Bobby's energy. He had hoped that his first operation would eliminate his dependency on the drugs he had taken for years, but instead he was forced to increase his daily dosage. He'd felt physically reborn after the first operation and had hoped the second wouldn't be necessary for at least five years. Now he feared that he would soon have to go under the knife again. "What the hell did I have the first operation for?" he raved. Reluctantly, he had added steroids to his list of medications and took them as prescribed. But early in 1973, when his health began to deteriorate anew, he questioned whether the drugs had served any purpose. He felt that the medications were causing him to lose control, and he didn't like the feeling . . . at all. "Why bother?" he thought, and tossed them in the trash.

One of these prescriptions was an anticoagulant called Coumadin, which allowed the blood to flow freely through his artificial valves. Like the others, it was a medicine Bobby would have to take for the rest of his life, and there would be serious repercussions if he stopped. Meanwhile, other problems were surfacing.

Anyone who has had open heart surgery or rheumatic fever must have massive doses of antibiotics to combat infection when any dental work is done. When Bobby went in to have his teeth cleaned his dentist didn't give him these antibiotics. An infection hit his bloodstream, and Bobby was admitted to Cedars of Lebanon Hospital with a serious case of blood poisoning.

Once there, complications set in. After he had experienced a series of mild strokes, the doctors discovered that Bobby had developed several small blood clots, or embolisms, on the brain. The strokes were no doubt a direct result of the embolisms—which in turn were caused by Bobby's decision to forego Coumadin. When the doctors realized what Bobby had done, they immediately put him back on all medications.

At Cedars, Bobby's heart went into arrest on a number of occasions, but each time he responded to emergency treatment. After a six-week stint, he was released, with the caution that he'd have to take it *very easy.*

Just a few days after Bobby's release from Cedars, while he and Andrea were visiting the Blauners for the evening, Bobby proposed. Completely surprised, Andrea begged for time—she wasn't sure what her answer would be. Bobby hadn't been himself lately, and she had begun to have her doubts about their future together. Bobby agreed to wait, but it wasn't long before the subject came up again.

A year or so before, Bobby had bought a tugboat and had spent a fortune having it turned into a houseboat. It was his pride and joy, and he took delight in acting as captain while Andrea and her boys served as crew. They had planned a boat trip up the Sacramento River for late June, and on the twenty-fifth of that month they arrived in Sausalito, where the boat was docked, to begin the cruise. With them were Andrea's two sons, Armin and Alex, and Bobby's son Dodd. After dropping the boys off at the dock, Bobby and Andrea headed for a grocery store to stock up on supplies for the two-week trip. On the way, he proposed again, and this time Andrea accepted. Within two minutes, Bobby had turned the car around and was on his way to the courthouse for a marriage license.

Blood tests had been done weeks before, when the question of marriage had first been broached. After getting the license, Bobby and Andrea drove to Walnut Grove, where they were married in the judge's chambers. As the news was released to the press, the couple stopped at the grocery store, picked up enough food for their trip, and returned to the boat.

Two weeks later, when they returned from their cruise, Bobby spoke to his lawyer, Gerald Lipsky, who tried to convince him that he should draw up a marital agreement. Bobby refused. He wouldn't ask any woman to start a marriage with such a pessimistic document hanging over her head. But only three days later, his attitude seemed to have changed. Bobby called Vee and told her that he already regretted the marriage. In the few weeks that he and Andrea had been man and wife, she'd brought up everything he'd ever done wrong. Every argument they'd never had, they had now. Andrea had kept her peace for three years; now she intended to let it all out. Although he loved Andrea deeply, he feared that their marriage had been a mistake.

Chapter Sixteen

"I think my number's up."

—Bobby Darin to Nina Cassotto Maffia,
October 1973.

On August 16, 1973, Bobby Darin made his last public appearance, a ten-day stint at the Las Vegas Hilton. He was so weak that by the end of each performance he was unable to leave the stage. Instead, when the curtain was rung down the stage hands would lead him, tired and shivering, to his dressing room, a pale shadow of his vital stage self.

On closing night, Vegas columnist Joe Delaney and his wife were in the audience. The Delaneys were close friends of Bobby's, but they didn't know how very sick he was—until that evening. One of the numbers in Bobby's act was James Taylor's poignant "Fire and Rain." While Bobby sang his emotional rendition of the song, the Delaneys found themselves holding hands. Suddenly it hit them—Bobby was sending them a message. As he reached the final line, "I always thought I would see you again," both the Delaneys and Bobby were in tears.

After the Hilton engagement, Bobby and Andrea left for a vacation in Micronesia. Ensconcing themselves in a small hotel, they lived on a diet

Bobby and Andrea in his dressing room at the Las Vegas Hilton shortly after their marriage in July 1973. This is the last known photograph taken of Bobby Darin.

that seemed to consist of nothing but peanut butter and eggs. Spending their days in a lush tropical jungle, they made occasional forays to nearby Guam to shop. On the way home to California, during a stopover in Hawaii, Bobby became seriously ill. His heart was again fibrillating, and he was retaining fluids. Quickly, they flew on to Los Angeles, and Bobby entered Cedars of Lebanon for immediate treatment.

The damage that had been detected during Bobby's earlier hospitalization was beginning to take its toll. Brain embolisms can have different effects depending on the part of the brain in which they are lodged. In June, Bobby had been told that the embolisms the doctors had found would eventually dissolve and pass. Until they did, he'd have to deal with the side effects.

Bobby's memory had begun to weaken. From time to time, he would have spells when he could remember everything that had happened to him in the past—but couldn't remember what he had just said. Often he would tell Andrea something three or four times. Mimi Greenberg, his former secretary and public relations representative, recalls that Bobby called to tell her that the William Morris office was arranging a syndicated radio program for him. He asked if Mimi would be interested in writing for the show and promised to be back in touch with her in a few days. When Mimi didn't hear from him, she called back to ask where the project stood. "I don't know what you're talking about," he told her. "I don't know anything about any radio show.'

"But Bobby," she protested, dumbfounded, "you called me yourself a week ago. You asked me if I'd help."

"You're crazy, and so is MacLean Stevenson," he snapped. "He just called and tried to tell me I'd asked him to be my opening act at the MGM Grand."

Mimi dropped the subject when she realized that Bobby was convinced that the earlier conversations had never taken place.

Bobby's attitude about his health was becoming surprisingly irrational and irresponsible. He was frightened by his lapses of memory and wanted help, but he was also reluctant to face the cause of his problem. He went from one doctor to another, paying attention to none. Each doctor he saw told him that extensive tests would have to be performed. Yet each time Bobby refused.

Most of Bobby's days were spent in seclusion. For hours at a time he would remain in a darkened bedroom, curled up in a fetal position, not even eating. Steve Blauner thought that Bobby was sinking fast, and he tried to reason with him. One afternoon, he walked into Bobby's bedroom, threw open the blinds, and turned to his friend. "You can still write fantastic music," he pleaded. "So what if you can't perform. You have so many other talents. Be grateful for that. You should consider yourself lucky that you have that ability."

Bobby wasn't interested. He had only really felt alive on stage. Without that, what was left? He thanked Steve for his concern and then simply asked him to close the blinds.

Before leaving, Blauner tried one more time. "Bobby," he begged, "please see someone. A shrink, a rabbi, a minister—anyone. Let someone help you." Bobby just shook his head and turned away.

But Blauner's advice did sink in. Some years earlier, Bobby had visited a psychiatrist in order to come to terms with his feelings about his unknown father and to seek help in dealing with his own son, Dodd. A few days after his visit, Steve Blauner received a call from Bobby. "I'm going to see a shrink," he explained. "I want you and Andrea to come with me." Blauner was overjoyed, but not for long. Nothing good came out of the session.

Depressed and feeling insecure, Bobby sat with Andrea and Blauner as the good doctor remarked casually, "Nothing's wrong with you from the neck down." The doctor proposed a period of observation in UCLA's psychiatric ward, with testing to begin as soon as possible. Andrea and Steve were grasping at straws, willing to do anything to get Bobby into the hospital.

Watching as his friend and wife nodded in agreement, Bobby couldn't believe what he was hearing. Blindly, he struck out at Andrea and Steve. "The two of you plotted this whole scheme to have me committed!" he screamed. Blauner reminded Bobby that he had made the appointment himself and that he and Andrea were only there at Bobby's request. Bobby left the office alone. Outside, he broke down and cried. There was something seriously wrong with him, but he knew he wasn't crazy. No, he was just scared—and terrified of what the tests would show. If his worst fears were confirmed and the end was near, he didn't know how he could accept it.

Just when he needed stability of some kind, Bobby's marriage with Andrea was on the rocks. Perhaps, he reasoned, divorcing Andrea would take the pressure off and restore the relationship. It would be a step back, but his world was closing in on him. He had no choice. Thus, on October 2, Bobby filed for a divorce from Andrea, rewriting his will to exclude her from any claim on his estate. On October 3, as Andrea was learning the news from his lawyer, Bobby was admitted to Cedars of Lebanon to be treated for congestive heart failure.

Now the fibrillations had reached a serious level. Bobby's heart would have to be stopped and restarted with shock treatments so that it would beat in the right rhythm. Coming out of the anesthetic afterwards, Bobby repeatedly thanked his doctors, Marvin Levy and Jack Fields. Fields corrected him, "Don't thank us, Bobby, thank God."

Bobby was amazed that he had made it through the procedure. Over and over again he asked, "Did it take? Did it take?" Then, speaking of his heart as if it were a separate being, he said, "It wants to take. It must have some sort of driving will to live. After thirty-seven years, it still wants to take."

On October 8, Bobby called Nina from the hospital. Not finding her at home, he managed to locate her at Vana's apartment in New York. Mother and son talked for hours. Bobby wept through most of the conversation. "I don't think I'm going to make it this time," he told her. "I think my number's up."

Bobby's voice seemed hollow and empty. Nina was worried; she'd never heard him sound so depressed. Summoning every ounce of optimism she could, she tried to reassure him. "Sweetheart, you're strong. You've always been stronger than we ever thought you were. You've lived through so much; you've got to live through this too."

Bobby told Nina of the confrontation with Andrea and Steve in the psychiatrist's office, of the sinking feeling he'd had as his wife and best friend agreed that he should put himself away. He sobbed uncontrollably as he remembered that horrible afternoon. He cried as Nina had never heard him cry before, as if he had held it in for years.

Nina tried another tack. "Sweetheart, are you having many visitors?"

"I've sent everyone away. I didn't want to see anyone."

Andrea and Steve were gone. He hadn't seen Dodd in weeks. He was alone. Just as he had predicted years before, the only people left were his family.

Moments after Nina hung up the phone, she had Vee Vee on the line. Bobby needed them. They must drive out to California immediately. Throwing a mattress and clothes into the back of Nina's station wagon, the two women started for Los Angeles. Less than forty-eight hours later, they were in Arizona. There they called Bobby from a telephone booth.

Bobby wasn't surprised to hear from them. "You know," he said, his voice cracking with emotion, "I just knew the two of you would come." He would be getting out of the hospital in a few days and would meet them in Las Vegas.

Two days later, Nina and Vee were at Bobby's home in Vegas when he let himself in the front door. As soon as he saw them he started to cry. At last, he had someone to hold on to. Even as they hugged and kissed him, his mother and sister were shocked by his appearance. His face was haggard, and he weighed no more than 120 pounds. His fine masculine hands were thin and emaciated. For a while, Bobby, Nina, and Vee just stood there, embracing each other, almost afraid to talk.

Although Bobby was obviously a very frail, very sick man, Nina somehow felt a certain awkwardness between herself and her son. He seemed to prefer Vee's company to her own, and often she would try to leave the two of them alone. He and Vee spent hours playing chess.

When Bobby and Nina were together, he argued with her constantly. He seemed to blame her for everything. And for the first time in his life, he expressed the bitterness he felt toward Polly, the woman he had so revered. After all, he pointed out, she too had lied to him. Most of what he was saying was the truth, or at least based on the truth, but he seemed unreasonably determined to argue the points with Nina.

Bobby's frustration about not knowing his father's identity had grown into fear. He suspected that he was coming down with Huntington's Chorea, a hereditary disease passed on from father to son that strikes men in their late twenties or mid-thirties. The symptoms included radical changes in personality, a jerky unsteady gait, and involuntary movements of the face, neck, and arms. Those who were with Bobby during this period do not recall any sign of these symptoms, save for personality changes—changes which could simply have been his reactions to his worsening heart condition and his fear of imminent death.

On October 23, Bobby visited his lawyer in Los Angeles to sign his new will. The entire estate was left to Dodd, with the provision that until his sixty-fifth birthday he would only get the income from the estate, not the principal. Until his twenty-first birthday, Dodd would be supported by funds from the estate. Bobby's lawyer, Gerald Lipsky, was named as the executor.

Bobby's motives behind the will were easy to understand. He didn't want to hand Dodd everything on a silver platter. To do this would be to rob him of any initiative. Without Bobby there to teach him the importance of setting his own goals and finding his own way, the unlimited funds could prove too much of a temptation; besides, his mother had expensive tastes.

Before leaving for Los Angeles to take care of the will, Bobby suggested that Nina also come to California. Vee was to wait for him in Vegas. A few days later, Gary flew out to Los Angeles and drove back to New York with Nina. The crisis had passed.

On October 24, Bobby appeared in a Las Vegas divorce court, accompanied by Kay Rozario, the wife of his longtime musical director. After the simple procedure, he rushed back to his house to call Andrea. But all he got was her answering service. "Tell her I got the divorce, and I hope she's satisfied," was his only message.

Bobby's state of mind had upset Kay, but she was careful to keep silent. However, once she had returned home, she rushed into her husband's arms, sobbing.

"Bobby's dying," she cried.

"Don't be foolish," Rozario replied, trying to fight off the obvious. "He'll be fine."

But Kay knew the truth, even if her husband refused to see it. She'd been with Bobby all day. His skin was cold and clammy. "He even smells of death," she sobbed.

Chapter Seventeen

"Cypress 2-6725."

—BOBBY DARIN'S FINAL WORDS, SPOKEN TO
VEE MAFFIA, DECEMBER 1973.

Now Bobby Darin was more scared than he had ever been in his entire life. He questioned just how much his heart could take; how often they could stop it and start it again. He was so tired. Years of abuse and the strain of his performances had taken their toll. He couldn't hold on much longer. The doctors wanted to catheterize his heart to find out more about his condition but, fearing their diagnosis, he refused. Instead, he went home for a brief rest.

Late in November, Bobby took a quick, somewhat surreptitious trip to New York to see a few friends. As much as he wanted to live, he was beginning to come to grips with the inevitable. He wanted a chance to bid farewell to the city where he had once roamed so freely and happily. He was only in New York a little more than twenty-four hours, and those friends he did seek out didn't realize he had come to say goodbye. They were disturbed by his deteriorating condition, but he avoided any discussion of the subject. He made no attempt to see Nina or the rest of his family. In fact, he didn't tell them of the trip until after his return to Los Angeles.

As Bobby grew weaker, he continued his farewells. Early in December, he visited his drummer, Tommy Amato, at his home. Tommy had been a young kid when Bobby discovered him and made him his drummer, and he had worked with Bobby steadily since 1968. Tommy hadn't seen his friend in a few months and was shocked by his appearance.

Bobby had brought a gift of liquor, the remains of his private stock. Tommy, wondering why Bobby wouldn't need it anymore, took the box and put it down in the corner of the hall. Then, turning to his friend, he fearfully asked him how he'd been feeling.

Bobby, avoiding the question, walked into the living room and settled down on the couch. When Amato noticed that Bobby was shivering, he covered him with a blanket. Other than the hellos, they had yet to speak. Suddenly, Bobby looked up at Tommy. "You know," he said, "we were supposed to open at the MGM Grand, but I'm not going to make it."

Amato was stunned. "We'll do the gig, and we'll have a great time," he stuttered. "Who are you kidding?"

But Bobby just shook his head sadly. "No, I'm gonna die, man. It's all over for me." The two men sat there a while longer, but small talk was impossible. Eventually, Bobby simply got up and left. They would never see each other again.

Although Bobby let down his guard with some of his friends, he continued to hide the seriousness of his condition from the press and the general public. "Everybody thinks I'm at death's door, but I'm not," he told one reporter. "There's nothing seriously wrong with me, and my heart is in a hundred percent working order. Anything else you may hear is a damn lie!" His denials must have been convincing because his illness was successfully kept under wraps, even during the most critical period.

Finally, on December 10, Bobby Darin realized that he could forestall the inevitable no longer. His heart fibrillations had become so serious that he could barely make his way to the bathroom without help. He called an ambulance and returned to the hospital to face the diagnosis: congestive heart failure.

Andrea spent much of that day and the next with him. She was shocked and saddened to find that Bobby's usual optimism had turned to an almost fatalistic acceptance of the inevitability of his death. She spent a great deal of time crying. Finally, Bobby sent her away. "If you can't stay with me without crying, if you can't be strong for me, then leave." She did so reluctantly.

On December 11, Bobby called his friend Larry Teacher, but reached Larry's wife, Marilynn. The two spoke for a while, but Marilynn found it hard to get Bobby to talk about anything in detail. He told her, of course, that he was in Cedars and admitted that he wasn't very well. Marilynn asked if he was having many visitors, and Bobby explained, somewhat sadly, that he had left word that he didn't want to see anyone. Then he asked what kind of a holiday the Teachers were planning. "A traditional family Christmas," Marilynn replied, and then added, "and we'd love for you to get better, get out of that hospital, and come spend the holiday with us."

Matter of factly, Bobby stated, "No, I won't be coming out of the hospital." Marilynn assumed that Bobby meant he wouldn't be out of the hospital in time for the holidays. What he was trying to tell her was that he didn't expect to make it this time.

On December 12, Vee received a telephone call from Bobby's lawyer, Gerald Lipsky.

"Get out here yesterday, your brother needs you."

Stunned, Vee asked, "What do you mean? What's wrong?"

"Don't ask questions, just get out here right away."

Vee flew to Los Angeles on the next available flight, arriving without a cent. She took a taxi to Lipsky's office, where he gave her some cash and the keys to Bobby's car, which she picked up at the house on Rodeo Drive. Then she drove to Cedars.

Vee spent every available hour at the hospital, holding Bobby's hand, talking to him, and comforting him. They cried together, they prayed together, and sometimes they even laughed together. In between, she did her best to keep Sandy and Dodd, as well as the rest of the family, up to date on Bobby's condition. Nina was told the facts, but Vee did her best to play down the gravity of the situation. Nina's heart had weakened considerably over the last few years, and Vee didn't want to do anything to endanger her mother's health. After Bobby's initial rebuff, Andrea made no attempt to see him at the hospital and never called.

Sitting there talking with Bobby, hour by hour, day by day, Vee grew to understand how desperately her brother wanted to live. He spent hours talking about his son and how much he wanted to play ball with him. At times, his despair would become violent, and he would cry out, cursing obscenities at God and mankind. He also prayed, with tears streaming down his face, that he might be allowed to live. Vee noticed a shocking change in Bobby's attitude since her last visit in October. Two months ago, he had wanted to live and was determined to make it. Now, although his will to live was just as strong, he didn't believe he would. He seemed to feel that he'd reached the point of no return.

Vee took it upon herself to fight for Bobby in the only way she knew how. She prayed, and with these prayers she convinced herself that her brother would live. For years, she felt she had stored up points with God, never asking for anything for herself. Now she prayed, asking that she be allowed to trade her points for Bobby's life. She firmly believed that there was no reason Bobby had to die. He was an extremely intelligent man, money was no problem, and he had the best doctors possible. What could go wrong?

Vee had so thoroughly convinced herself that Bobby wouldn't die that she spent her first few days at the hospital trying to find out whether he could be released before Christmas so that she could plan a special dinner for him. The doctors were speaking in terms of "when he recovers," and this also helped to give Vee hope. She continually, relentlessly tried to convince Bobby that everything would be all right and forced him to make plans for his future. She was thrilled when he agreed to return with her to her home in the Catskills, where he could recover in peace and quiet.

Throughout this period, Bobby's heartbeat was extremely erratic. Most days were spent in bed, yet he was constantly exhausted. It took a superhuman effort for him to make his way to the bathroom.

Bobby didn't want any visitors other than Vee. Dodd and Sandy had been forbidden to see him, and even his best friends weren't allowed in. It hurt him to see strong, healthy people; he envied their health. Vee recalls few attempts on anyone's part to visit Bobby and almost no telephone calls. Of course, Blauner and Gershenson, manager and press agent, were kept informed.

One day, Richard Bakalayan and Gary Wood came to the hospital, begging to see Bobby. Vee explained to Bobby how upset and insistent the two men were. Finally, Bobby agreed to let them in. Though shocked by his appearance, they tried to bolster his sagging spirits. Bobby could only reply, "I love you. Forgive me, but I don't want to see you." He sent them away. In the hall outside his room, they broke down and cried.

By December 16, Bobby was hovering near death. It was Dodd's birthday, and Bobby asked Vee to bring a note to his son. No one felt much like celebrating, but nevertheless, Vee and Mary Douvan joined Sandy and Dodd that day for a small party. The birthday cake was barely touched. Sandy was devastated by Bobby's ever-worsening condition and wanted desperately to visit him, but Mary and Vee wouldn't hear of it. Sandy spent most of the day crying. She missed Bobby and had never wanted to be married to anyone else. For years, she had held on to the hope that they might reconcile, and now she was faced with the fact that it was never to be. The only man she had ever really loved lay in the hospital dying. She wanted to sit by his bed, hold his hand, and tell him everything would be okay, and they wouldn't let her near his room.

Suddenly, there was a telephone call for Dodd from his father. Dodd got on the line, but Bobby wasn't making much sense. His death was imminent, he cried bitterly. He wouldn't live to see his son grow up. For the first time, Dodd was fully aware of the impending tragedy. He wanted to run away and cry, but he also wanted to talk to his father.

Sandy was standing by him and realized that whatever Bobby was saying was upsetting their son. Gently, she took the receiver out of his hand and tried to talk to Bobby herself—but by this point, he wasn't speaking coherently. She too became scared and more upset.

Vee took the telephone and tried to calm her brother down. "Bobby, you're not going to die. You're not going to die," she repeated, over and over again. Once he had regained some self-control, she said, "Now, hang on. Hang on real tight, because I'm on my way."

Bobby replied, "All right, all right. But tell Dodd I love him." Then he hung up.

While Vee was speaking to Bobby, Dodd had written his father a note. As she rushed out to the car, he ran after her, waving it in his hand. Taking the note, she roared off into the night as Dodd returned to Sandy, who was now fully aware that her world was crumbling around her.

Before Vee reached the hospital, Bobby had placed another call, this time to Andrea. "This is it," he said. "I'm not going to make it. I really love you, but I'm going to die."

When Vee arrived, she found Bobby sinking fast, rambling incoherently. For two days, he hovered between life and death. At one point, he told her, "Save Dodd from the wolves."

As he lay there tossing and turning in discomfort, Bobby couldn't help but remember his childhood—and Polly. He and Polly had been so full of hopes back then. They had had so many dreams and, in the end, most of them had come true. Slowly, a smile came to his face as he remembered the warmth and love he had felt in her presence.

Then, turning to Vee, he said clearly, "Cypress 2-6725."

Vee went wide-eyed with wonder. It had been their first telephone number, over twenty years before, in the Bronx. Bobby had been so excited when it was installed. "Bobby, do you know what you're saying?" she gasped.

Bobby just continued to smile as he put his finger to his lips, "Shhh." Then he repeated the number and closed his eyes as he sank into a coma. It was December 18, 1973.

Soon after, Bobby's heart stopped beating. The doctors managed to revive him quickly with electroshock treatments, but he still remained comatose. Until this time, the doctors had continued to plead with him to allow a catheterization of his heart, which he'd refused. Now Bobby was unconscious, and the situation was out of his hands. The doctors appealed to Vee, and she gave her consent. If there was any possibility that they could help him, Vee wanted Bobby to have that chance.

Faced with complete responsibility for her brother's care, Vee's morale began to weaken. She wasn't sure she could hold out alone anymore. In desperation, she called Gerald Lipsky, Bobby's lawyer. Lipsky arrived while the catheterization was taking place. As Vee explained the situation, Lipsky began to turn white. Shaking his head and running to the door, Lipsky responded, "I wish I could help you, but I can't take it. I simply can't take it." Once again, Vee was alone with her brother.

The results of the catheterization showed that one of the valves in Bobby's heart was malfunctioning and would have to be replaced, but there was some question whethr he was strong enough to withstand the operation. The doctors told Vee that they would wait until the next day; if Bobby lived through the night, he would be somewhat stronger and might be able to withstand the ordeal. The doctors and nurses tried to talk Vee into going home to rest but, just as she had all week, she declined, remaining with Bobby through the night.

Vee had had several telephone conversations with Nina and Charlie throughout the day. Both had offered to come out and stay with her, but she had managed to talk them out of it. When Richard Behrke called from New York, she wasn't as successful.

Behrke called at a point when Vee's composure and strength were at their lowest ebb. When she explained her own desperate mental state, he was overcome. He had known Bobby longer than most and loved him like a brother. "Should I come out there? Do you want me out there?" he asked her.

Vee could hold out no longer. She didn't have the heart or the strength to refuse. She needed someone to share the burden. Tearfully, she told him, "Dickie, I think if you ever want to see Bobby again, you'd betteer come out right away."

Bobby did survive the night. At 9:30 on the morning of December 19, he was taken into the operating room, still unconscious. Before letting him go, Vee gave him a quick kiss and a hug, and then made the sign of the cross. It had been a week full of prayers, and now she was praying harder than ever.

Once Bobby was opened up, the doctors found that the left side of his heart was infected. Too much of the heart had been cut away during the first operation to allow much more to be done now, but still they worked feverishly to remove the infection and replace the malfunctioning valve. Bobby was being kept alive by a heart and lung machine. His chances of survival were slim.

Meanwhile, Vee was joined by David Gershenson and Richard Behrke. Together they paced, prayed, and cried, hoping that somehow Bobby would survive one more time. Finally, the operation was completed. Bobby's heart was still being massaged electronically, and it would be a while before the doctors would know if it would adapt well enough to beat on its own. Eventually, Bobby's heart rallied, and he was taken off the machinery. It seemed that he might be able to survive.

Now that his heart was beating on its own, the doctors waited for Bobby to regain consciousness. Vee, David, and Dick remained in the waiting room, afraid to allow themselves to believe that Bobby would be all right. Vee was functioning on pure nervous energy; she had been awake for two straight days.

After midnight, Bobby took a turn for the worse. He'd regained consciousness when he had come out of the anesthesia and had become hysterical. Then his heart stopped and was started again. He was being kept alive by the electronic heart massager. To make matters worse, when his heart stopped, his kidneys had failed. There had also been brain damage. His heart was simply too weak to beat on its own. The massager was the only thing keeping him alive, and even that wouldn't work much longer.

A transplant was out. For all intents and purposes, Bobby was dead.

The doctors could wait until the machine was no longer effective, or they could pull the plug. It was both the hardest and easiest decision Vee would ever make. "Pull the plug," Vee said, tears coursing down her face.

When the doctors left, Vee went numb. David Gershenson broke down in tears. Richard Behrke, trying hard not to cry, sat there with his eyes getting redder and redder. Vee, trembling with pent-up emotion, refused to give in to her grief. Pulling herself together with one last burst of hidden strength, she told Gershenson, who was preparing to call the press, "You will call no one until I have called my mother and Sandra." Gershenson acquiesced.

Vee called Nina and then tried to call Mary Douvan, but got no response. Then she tried Sandy's number, but got no answer there either. Reluctantly, she gave Dave Gershenson the go-ahead to make a public announcement of Bobby's death. Then Vee, Behrke, and Gershenson headed for Sandy's home. On the way, Vee finally collapsed, and Behrke and Gershenson dropped her off at Bobby's home. Meanwhile, the news of Bobby's death had been broadcast over radio and television, and Mary Douvan had heard it. She too rushed to her daughter's home.

When Dick and David arrived at Sandy's Mary was already there. Mary had arrived to find the lights out and doors locked. After getting no answer at the door, she had broken into a garage window. Inside, she found Sandy and Dodd, both asleep. She had just awakened them with the news of Bobby's death when the two men arrived.

Shortly after three A.M., the telephone rang in Nina Cassotto's bedroom, waking both her and Gary. As soon as he heard the sound, Gary knew what had happened. Moments later, Nina's screams shattered the night. "He didn't make it. He's dead!" Then, running to Gary, she burst into tears.

Cradling his mother in his arms, Gary could feel the tears running down her face against his own. "He didn't make it," she sobbed over and over, "Oh God, he didn't make it."

Nina cried far into the morning hours. She cried for Bobby, dead at thirty-seven; she cried for her mother, who she missed so much and who had meant so much to Bobby; and she cried for herself because she had lost her son again. Once, years before, she had given him up willingly, hoping that it would mean a better life for him. Now, he had been taken from her once more, permanently.

She remembered his words. "You'll always love me Nina, won't you? I could do anything to you, and you'd still love me. Even if I was broke, I could still come home to you."

"Yes Bobby," she thought, "I'll always love you. Nina will always love you, sweetheart. I'll always love you . . . son."

—♪—

Epilogue

Bobby Darin left explicit instructions in his last will and testament for the disposition of his remains. There was to be no viewing and no burial service. His body was left to medical research. But the rituals of wakes and funerals serve a valuable purpose in the long run; they formalize the end of a life and grant those who knew the deceased an opportunity to recognize his passing and to accept his death publicly. In the absence of these ceremonies, Bobby's friends and family had to come to terms with his passing privately, and in many cases this was no simple matter. Years later, those closest to Bobby are still finding it hard to cope with his death. The absence of that presence has created a vacuum that to many remains unfilled.

Larry Teacher traveled in Bobby's world for just a short period of time. He, possibly more than anyone else, was a friend of Bob Darin, the man, and not Bobby Darin, the celebrity. Nevertheless, it took almost ten years for him to be able to hear Bobby's music without being upset. The chess board on which he and Bobby often played remains untouched in his home. The publication of this book is Larry's own tribute to the man he and his wife Marilynn took into their hearts and home just a few years before his death.

For years after Bobby's death, Nina Cassotto found it nearly impossible to hear Bobby's music or see his movies on television. Unable to put him out of her mind, she prayed for help, and her cooperation in the writing of this book was her own way of accepting the facts of Bobby's life, his attitude toward her, and his untimely death. Until her death in November of 1983 she lived a quiet life in northern New Jersey, finding comfort in the presence of her younger son, Gary, who cared for her "like a treasure."

Vee Vee Walden, Bobby's oldest sister and the one person to remain with him throughout his final illness, lives alone in Calicoon, New York. Her deep and abiding love for her brother has remained. Nevertheless, she continues to wrestle with the contradictions in Bobby's personality and his reluctance to accept Nina as his mother and she, Vana, and Gary as his sisters and brother. Even so, just the simple utterance of the words "my brother" seems to bring a lump to her throat.

It is said that Steve Blauner, Bobby's former manager and once one of Bobby's closest friends, still speaks of him in the present tense. It is also said that he carries a print of Bobby's last television show with him everywhere he goes and views it often.

Richard behrke, Bobby's oldest and dearest friend, who was with Vee when Bobby died, still has trouble talking about him. Nevertheless, he and his wife Mickie treat Bobby's memory with the kind of integrity and respect that can only come from the most sincere affection.

Bobby's wives, Andrea and Sandra, seem to be haunted by his life as well as his death. Andrea married Bobby's longtime friend and business associate, Steve Burton, Ed Burton's son. Sandra Dee, once one of Hollywood's biggest stars and perhaps the greatest love of Bobby's life, lives with their son Dodd in Beverly Hills. Although it is said that she could have a television series of her own any time she wishes, she has all but retired since 1970 and has never remarried or been romantically linked with another.

The Curtain Falls

MUSIC AND LYRICS WRITTEN FOR BOBBY DARIN BY SOL WEINSTEIN.

Off comes the greasepaint,
Off comes the clown's disguise.
The curtain's falling,
The music softly dies.

I hope you're smiling
As you're filing out the door.
They say in show biz, that's all there is.
There isn't anymore.

We've shared a moment,
And as the magic ends,
I've got a feeling
We're parting now as friends.

Your cheers and laughter
Will linger after
They've torn down these dusty walls.

People say I was made for this,
Nothing else would I trade for this,
And to think I get paid for this.

But now the curtain falls.

Bobby Darin on Record

1956

SINGLES

Decca *9-29883* Rock Island Line/Timber

Decca *9-29922* Silly Willy/Blue Eyed Mermaid

Decca *9-30031* Hear Them Bells/The Greatest Builder

1957

SINGLES

Decca *9-30225* Dealer in Dreams/Help Me

Atco *6092* I Found a Million Dollar Baby/Talk to Me Something

Atco *6103* Don't Call My Name/Pretty Betty

1958

SINGLES

Atco *6109* Just in Case You Change Your Mind/So Mean

Atco *6117* Splish Splash/Judy Don't Be Moody

Atco *6121* Early in the Morning/Now We're One

Atco *6127* Queen of the Hop/Lost Love

Atco *6128* Mighty Mighty Man/You're Mine

ALBUMS

Atco *33-102* BOBBY DARIN *(Released July, 1958)*

Splish Splash; Just in Case You Change Your Mind; Pretty Betty; Talk to Me Something; Judy, Don't Be Moody; (Since You've Been Gone) I Can't Go On; I Found a Million Dollar Baby (In a Five and Ten Cent Store); Wear My Ring; So Mean; Don't Call My Name; Brand New House; Actions Speak Louder Than Words

1959

SINGLES

Atco *6133* Plain Jane/While I'm Gone

Atco *6140* Dream Lover/Bullmoose

Atco *6147* Mack the Knife/Was There a Call For Me

ALBUMS

Atco *33-104* THAT'S ALL *(Recorded December 19, 22, 24, 1958. Released March 1959.)*

Mack the Knife; Beyond the Sea; Through a Long and Sleepless Night; Softly as in a Morning Sunrise; She Needs Me; It Ain't Necessarily So; I'll Remember April; That's the Way Love Is; Was There a Call For Me?;

Some of These Days;
Where is the One; That's
All

1960

SINGLES

Atco	6158	Beyond the Sea/That's the Way Love Is
Atco	6161	Clementine/Tall Story
Atco	SPD	Moment of Love/She's Tanfastic
Atco	6167	Bill Bailey/I'll Be There
Atco	6173	Beachcomber/Autumn Blues
Atco	6179	Artificial Flowers/ Somebody to Love
Atco	6183	Christmas Auld Lang Syne/Child of God
Colpix	CP1	That's How It Went All Right/(non-Darin flip side)

ALBUMS

Atco	33-115	THIS IS DARIN *(Recorded May 19-21, 1959. Released January, 1960.)* Have You Got Any Castles Baby?; Don't Dream of Anybody But Me; My Gal Sal; Black Coffee; Caravan; Guys and Dolls; Down With Love; Pete Kelly's Blues; All Nite Long; The Gal That Got Away; I Can't Give You Anything But Love
Atco	33-122	DARIN AT THE COPA *(Recorded June 15-16,*

1960. Released July, 1960.) Swing Low Sweet Chariot; Lonesome Road; Some of These Days; Mack the Knife; Love for Sale; Clementine; You'd Be So Nice to Come Home To; Dream Lover; Bill Bailey; I Have Dreamed; I Can't Give You Anything But Love; Alright, OK, You Win; By Myself; When Your Lover Has Gone; I Got a Woman; That's All

Atco	SP-1001	FOR TEENAGERS ONLY *(Released September, 1960.)* I Want You with Me; Keep a Walkin'; You Know How; Somebody to Love; I Ain't Sharin' Sharon; Pity Miss Kitty; That Lucky Old Sun; All the Way Home; You Never Called; A Picture No Artist Could Paint; Hush, Somebody's Calling My Name; Here I'll Stay
Atco	33-125	THE 25TH DAY OF DECEMBER *(Recorded June 19–21, 1960. Released October, 1960.)* O Come All Ye Faithful; Poor Little Jesus; Child of God; Baby Born Today; Holy Holy Holy; Ave Maria; Go Tell It On the Mountain; While the Shepherds Watched their

Flocks; Jehovah
Hallelujah; Mary, Where is
Your Baby; Silent Night;
Dona Nobis Pacem; Amen

1961

SINGLES

Atco	6188	Lazy River/Oo-Ee-Train
Atco	6196	Nature Boy/Look For My True Love
Atco	6200	Theme from *Come September*/Walk Back to Me
Atco	6206	You Must Have Been a Beautiful Baby/Sorrow Tomorrow
Atco	6211	Ave Maria/O Come All Ye Faithful
Atco	6214	Irresistible You/ Multiplication

ALBUMS

Atco 33-126 BOBBY DARIN & JOHNNY MERCER: TWO OF A KIND *(Recorded August 13-22, 1960. Released February, 1961.)*

Two of a Kind; Indiana; Bob White; Ace in the Hole; East of the Rockies; If I Had My Druthers; I Ain't Gonna Give Nobody None of My Jellyroll; Lonesome Polecat; My Cutie's Due at Two-To-Two Today; Paddlin' Madelin' Home/Row Row Row; Who Takes Care of the Caretaker's Daughter?;

Mississippi Mud; Two of a Kind (reprise)

Atco 33-134 LOVE SWINGS *(Recorded 21-23, 1961. Released July, 1961.)*

Long Ago and Far Away; I Didn't Know What Time it Was; How About You?; The More I See You; It Had to Be You; No Greater Love; In Love In Vain; Just Friends; Something to Remember You By; Skylark; Spring Is Here; I Guess I'll Have To Change My Plan

Atco 33-138 TWIST WITH BOBBY DARIN *(Released December, 1961)*

Bullmoose; Early in the Morning; Mighty Mighty Man; You Know How; Somebody to Love; Multiplication; Irresistible You; Queen of the Hop; You Must Have Been a Beautiful Baby; Keep A Walkin'; Pity Miss Kitty; I ain't Sharin' Sharon

1962

SINGLES

Atco	6211	What'd I Say? (Part I); What'd I Say? (Part II)
Atco	6229	Things/Jailer Bring Me Water
Capitol	4837	If A Man Answers/A True True Love

Atco	*6236*	Baby Face/You Know How
Atco	*6244*	I Found a New Baby/Keep a Walkin'

ALBUMS

Atco *33-140* BOBBY DARIN SINGS RAY CHARLES *(Released March, 1962.)*
What'd I Say?; I Got a Woman; Tell All the World About You; Tell Me How You Feel; My Bonnie; The Right Time; Hallelujah I Love Her So; Leave My Woman Alone; Ain't That Love; Drown In My Own Tears; That's Enough

Atco *33-146* THINGS & OTHER THINGS *(Released July, 1962)*
Things; I'll Be There; Lost Love; Look For My True Love; Beachcomber; Now We're One; You're Mine; Oo-Ee-Train; Jailer Bring Me Water; Nature Boy; Theme from *Come September*; Sorrow Tomorrow

Capitol *1791* OH! LOOK AT ME NOW *(Recorded July, 1962. Released October, 1962)*
All By Myself; My Buddy; There's a Rainbow 'Round My Shoulder; Roses of Picardy; You'll Never Know; Blue Skies; Always; You Made Me Love You; A Nightingale Sang in Berkeley Square; I'm Beginning to See the Light; Oh! Look at Me Now; The Party's Over

1963
SINGLES

Capitol	*4897*	You're the Reason I'm Living/Now You're Gone
Capitol	*4970*	18 Yellow Roses/Not For Me
Capitol	*5019*	Treat My Baby Good/Down So Long
Capitol	*5079*	Be Mad Little Girl/Since You've Been Gone

ALBUMS

Capitol *1866* YOU'RE THE REASON I'M LIVING *(Recorded January, 1963. Released February, 1963)*
Sally Was a Good Old Girl; Be Honest with Me; Oh Lonesome Me; (I Heard that) Lonesome Whistle; It Keeps Right on a Hurtin'; You're The Reason I'm Living; Please Help Me I'm Falling; Under Your Spell Again; Here I Am; Who Can I Count On?; Now You're Gone; Release Me

Atco *33-124* IT'S YOU OR NO ONE *(Recorded January 25-27, 1960. Released June, 1963.)*

It's You Or No One; I Hadn't Anyone Till You; Not Mine; I Can't Believe That You're in Love With Me; I've Never Been in Love Before; All or Nothing At All; Only One Little Item; Don't Get Around Much Anymore; How About Me?; I'll Be Around; All I Do Is Cry; I Guess I'm Good For Nothing But the Blues

Capitol *1942* 18 YELLOW ROSES (Released July, 1963)

18 Yellow Roses; On Broadway; Ruby Baby; Reverend Mr. Black; End of the World; Not For Me; Walk Right In; From a Jack to a King; I Will Follow Her; Our Day Will Come; Can't Get Used to Losing You; Rhythm of the Rain

Capitol *1826* EARTHY! (*Recorded July, 1962. Released July, 1963.*)

Long Time Man; Work Song; La Bamba; I'm On My Way Great God; The Sermon of Samson; Strange Rain; Why Don't You Swing Down; Everything's Okay; Guantanamera; When Their Mama Is Gone; Fay-O; The Er-i-ee Was A'Rising

Capitol *2007* GOLDEN FOLK HITS (*Released November, 1963.*)

Mary Don't You Weep; Where Have All the Flowers Gone?; If I Had a Hammer; Don't Think Twice; Greenback Dollar; Why Daddy Why; Michael Row the Boat Ashore; Abilene; Green, Green; Settle Down (Goin' Down That Highway); Blowin' in the Wind; Train to the Sky

1964
SINGLES

Capitol *5126* I Wonder Who's Kissing Her Now/As Long As I'm Singing

Atco *6297* Milord/Golden Earrings

Atco *6316* Swing Low Sweet Chariot/Similar

Capitol *5257* The Things in This House/Wait By the Water

ALBUMS

Capitol *2194* FROM HELLO DOLLY TO GOODBYE CHARLIE (*Released November, 1964*)

Hello Dolly!; Call Me Irresponsible; The Days of Wine and Roses; More; The End of Never; Charade; Once in a Lifetime; Sunday in New York; Where Love Has Gone; Look at Me; Goodbye, Charlie

1965

SINGLES

Capitol	5359	Hello Dolly/Goodbye Charlie
Capitol	5399	Venice Blue/In a World Without You
Capitol	5443	When I Get Home/Lonely Road
Capitol	5481	That Funny Feeling/Gyp the Cat
Atco	6334	Minnie the Moocher/Hard Hearted Hannah
Atlantic	2305	We Didn't Ask to Be Brought Here/Funny What Love Can Do

ALBUMS

| Capitol | 2322 | VENICE BLUE *(Released May, 1965)* |

Venice Blue; I Wanna Be Around; Somewhere; The Good Life; Dear Heart; Softly As I Leave You; You Just Don't Know; There Ain't No Sweet Gal That's Worth the Salt of My Tears; Who Can I Turn To?; A Taste of Honey; In a World Without You

Songs Written By Bobby Darin

Bobby Darin was one of the first superstar singer-songwriters . . . a forerunner of such performers as Billy Joel, Barry Manilow, and Carole King. Beginning in 1956 and through the end of his career, Darin wrote and published almost 200 songs. More often than not he was responsible for both the words and music, however, his occasional collaborators included such names as Don Kirshner, Terry Melcher, Woody Harris, and Johnny Mercer. In 1958, disc jockey Murray "the K" Kaufman's mother suggested that Bobby write a song entitled "Splish Splash." Bobby took the challenge and wrote what would become one of rock and roll's most legendary hits—and he wrote it in less than an hour.

Following is a list of all songs for which Bobby Darin is the registered copyright owner. Those songs in boldface were also recorded by Bobby Darin. (See the Discography for further information about these recordings.)

SONG TITLE	COLLABORATOR	COPYRIGHT DATE
After School Rock and Roll	Don Kirshner/George M. Shaw	3/21/56
All Your Friends Are Here		4/14/67
Amy		1/27/67
Another Song On My Mind	Tommy Amato	3/11/74
As Long As I'm Singing		8/28/62
Autumn Blues		8/9/60
Baby I Miss You		9/15/65
Baby May		*12/29/69*
Bad Girl		4/4/63
Ballet Dance		4/14/67
Barbara Ann	Claire Kaufman	4/2/58
Be Mad Little Girl		9/18/63
Beachcomber		8/9/60
Bi-aza-ku-sasa	Rudi Trailor	7/11/58
Boss Barracuda	Terry Melcher	5/22/64
Brand New House	*Woody Harris*	*7/30/58*

SONG TITLE	COLLABORATOR	COPYRIGHT DATE
Broken Up Inside	David Hill	3/17/60
Bubble Gum Pop	Don Kirshner	1/17/56
Bullfrog		**8/10/68**
Bullmoose		**4/9/58**
By My Side	Don Kirshner	7/22/57
Can't You See Me?		4/14/67
Casey, Wake Up		5/12/64
Change		*8/9/68*
Chantal's Theme		6/21/62
Coffee Perkin' Time		10/7/64
Come		4/14/67
Come September (Instrumental)		*6/1/61*
Come September (with lyric)	Cy Cohen	11/2/66
Comin' Down with a Heartache	Rudy Clark	4/15/63
Daydreamer	Jimmy Boyd	5/1/62
Dealer in Dreams	*Don Kirshner*	*4/24/56*
Delia	Don Kirshner	4/3/57
Distractions		**6/6/69**
Don't Call My Name	**Don Kirshner**	**10/21/57**
Down So Long		**7/25/63**
Dream Baby	Arthur Resnick	9/25/63
Dream Lover		**4/9/59**
Early in the Morning	**Woody Harris**	**6/9/58**
Eighteen Yellow Roses		**4/22/63**
Elizabeth		12/13/63
The End of Never	*Francine Forest*	*7/31/64*
Everywhere I Go		1/18/63
Face to Face		4/14/67
The Feelin'	David Hill	3/17/60
Fourteen Pairs of Shoes	Russell Alquist	4/9/65
Freedom to Love	Arthur Resnick	2/12/64
Funny What Love Can Do		*9/15/65*
Gone		12/26/62
The Great Society		2/3/65

SONG TITLE	COLLABORATOR	COPYRIGHT DATE
The Greatest Lover in the World		4/14/67
Gyp the Cat	Don Wolf	7/29/65
The Harvest		6/6/69
Hello Sunshine		4/7/67
Hey Magic Man		6/6/69
Hot Rod U.S.A.	Terry Melcher	4/13/64
I Am		4/7/67
I Can See the Wind		8/9/68
I Can't Believe a Word You Say	Rudy Clark	5/15/63
I Want to Spend Christmas With Elvis	Don Kirshner	11/28/56
I Got My Own Thing Going	Rudy Clark	7/29/65
I'll Be There		10/20/59
I'm Gonna Love You		1/18/68
If You Love Him		3/12/64
If a Man Answers		6/21/62
In Memoriam		8/9/68
It's Him I Want To Go With Mama	Arthur Resnick	4/20/64
It's What's Happening Baby		6/14/65
Jailer, Bring Me Water		6/12/62
Jingle Jangle Jingle		8/9/68
Jive		6/6/69
Keep-A-Movin' Mama	Don Kirshner	2/11/57
Light Blue		6/6/69
The Lively Set		3/23/64
Long Time Movin'		1/18/68
Long Line Rider		8/9/68
Look At Me	Randy Newman	6/25/64
Look For My True Love		6/24/60
Los Angeles	Francine Forest	8/4/66
Lost Love	Don Kirshner	8/6/58
Love Me Right	Don Kirshner	7/23/57
Made in the Shade		5/1/62

SONG TITLE	COLLABORATOR	COPYRIGHT DATE
Maybe We Can Make It Together		3/2/70
Me & Mr. Hohner		5/12/69
Mighty Mighty Man		10/24/58
Moment of Love		10/8/59
Monkey	Rudy Clark	6/18/63
Moment of Love	Don Kirshner	2/7/58
Multiplication		*8/15/61*
My First Real Love	Don Kirshner/George M. Shaw	2/15/56
My Dog Got a Tag On Her		11/19/64
My Mom	Terry Melcher	8/22/64
Not For Me		*4/22/63*
Now We're One		*6/9/58*
OK Girl (aka OK Boy)	Russell Alquist	4/16/65
Oo-ee Train		*2/2/62*
Peck-a-Cheek	Cy Cohen	517/58
Prescription Fire (aka RX-Pyro)		*3/2/70*
Pretty Betty	*Don Kirshner*	*10/21/57*
Prisoner of Your Love		1/18/68
The Proper Gander		8/9/68
Queen of the Hop	**Woody Harris**	8/29/58
Questions		8/9/68
Rainin'		4/7/66
Real Love	Woody Harris	6/11/58
The Rest of My Life		4/2/58
Revolution of the Goats	Norman Strassberg	8/6/58
Rock Pile	Don Kirshner/George M. Shaw	3/14/56
The Rogers Cha Cha	Don Kirshner	2/6/56
Run Little Rabbit		4/13/64
Sausalito (The Governor's Song)		*6/6/69*
Save a Sinking Heart	Al Byron	1/26/61
School's Out	Woody Harris	6/11/58
She's Tanfastic		*5/6/60*
Shirl Girl	Rudy Clark	9/25/63
Silly Willy	*Don Kirshner/George M. Shaw*	*3/14/56*

SONG TITLE	COLLABORATOR	COPYRIGHT DATE
Simple Song of Freedom		*6/12/69*
So Mean	Don Kirshner	7/3/57
Somebody to Love		10/20/59
Something in Her Love	Tommy Amato	10/31/72
Somewhere Out There		4/14/67
Song For a Dollar		*5/12/69*
Soul City		8/7/64
Splish Splash	*Jean Murray*	*6/6/58*
Sugar Man		12/5/66
Sugar Man		6/6/69
Summertime Symphony		6/22/59
Sunday		8/9/58
Sweet Reasons		12/29/69
Talk To Me Something	Don Kirshner	2/14/67
That Funny Feeling		10/12/64
That's The Way Love Is		*4/2/58*
Things		9/8/61
The Things in This House		8/26/64
This Little Girl's Gone Rockin'	Manny Curtis	4/25/58
Three to Get Ready		3/23/61
Timber	Don Kirshner/George M. Shaw	3/12/56
Treat My Baby Good		*7/25/63*
A True True Love		8/28/62
Turbine Montage		10/7/64
Turned Down Theme		3/2/64
Two of a Kind	*Johnny Mercer*	*12/8/60*
Two Tickets		10/12/64
Wait a Minute	Don Kirshner	1/12/61
Wait By the Water		8/26/64
Walk Back to Me		7/11/61
Water Color Canvas		6/6/69
We Didn't Ask to Be Brought Here		9/15/65
Wear My Ring	Don Kirshner	4/30/57

SONG TITLE	COLLABORATOR	COPYRIGHT DATE
Wendy		12/3/64
Wat'cha You Mean	Rudi Trailor	7/11/58
When I Get Home	Russell Alquist	5/12/65
While I'm Gone		*2/18/63*
Whomp Be Omp Bomp		6/13/58
Why Oh You	Don Kirshner	2/21/57
Wilco Jingle	Don Kirshner	2/6/56
A World Without You	**Rudy Clark**	**3/22/65**
You Just Don't Know		**3/22/65**
You Know How		**10/8/59**
You Got Me		4/14/67
You're the Reason I'm Living		*12/26/62*
You're Mine		*10/24/58*
Zoon-A-Roo	Arthur Resnick	3/9/64

Bobby Darin's Television Appearances

Throughout the seventeen years of Bobby Darin's career (1956–1973) he was a popular guest on television variety and drama shows as well as the host of several variety specials and his own TV series. The following list identifies almost one hundred such appearances. It is not necessarily complete. All of Darin's many appearances on *American Bandstand,* for instance, are missing. Also missing are Bobby's appearances on *The Tonight Show* as well as other talk show appearances and local television appearances.

Whenever possible this list includes all of Bobby's songs from each performance. Again, the list is not complete in this respect. In some cases there is no information available—in other cases the information available about a given show may be incomplete. Nevertheless, I have included all available data.

Stage Show—March 10, 1956—CBS
Hosted by the Dorsey Brothers. Bobby's songs included The Rock Island Line.

The Big Beat—July 19, 1957—New York City local television
Hosted by Alan Freed. Bobby's songs included Talk To Me Something.

The Dick Clark Beechnut Show—July 19, 1958—ABC
Hosted by Dick Clark. Bobby's songs included Splish Splash.

The Bob Crosby Show—August 23, 1958—NBC
Hosted by Bob Crosby. Bobby's songs included Splish Splash.

The Dick Clark Beechnut Show—November 1, 1958—ABC
Hosted by Dick Clark. Bobby's songs included Queen Of The Hop.

The Dick Clark Beechnut Show—January 10, 1959—ABC
Hosted by Dick Clark. Bobby's songs are unknown.

The Perry Como Show—NBC
Hosted by Perry Como. Bobby's songs are unknown.

The Dick Clark Beechnut Show—May 2, 1959—CBS

Hosted by Dick Clark. Bobby's songs included Dream Lover.

The Ed Sullivan Show—May 31, 1959—CBS

Hosted by Ed Sullivan. Bobby's songs included Mack The Knife and Dream Lover.

The Big Beat—July 9, 1959—New York City local television

Guest Host: Bobby Darin. Bobby did not sing during this appearance.

The Dick Clark Beechnut Show—August 22, 1959—ABC

Hosted by Dick Clark. Bobby's songs included Mack The Knife and Dream Lover.

The Ed Sullivan Show—September 6, 1959—CBS

Hosted by Ed Sullivan. Bobby's songs included Clementine and By Myself.

An Evening With Jimmy Durante—September 25, 1959—NBC

Hosted by Jimmy Durante. Bobby's songs included: Mack The Knife, That's All, Bill Bailey (with Durante) and Personality (with Durante).

Hennesey—October 5, 1959—CBS

Drama series starring Jackie Cooper. Bobby Darin's character was called Honeyboy Jones. The episode was entitled "Hennesey Meets Honeyboy."

The Louis Jourdan Timex Special—November 11, 1959—NBC

Hosted by Louis Jourdan. Bobby's songs are unknown.

George Burns in the Big Time—November 17, 1959—NBC

Hosted by George Burns. Bobby's songs included Clementine and I Ain't Got Nobody (with Burns).

This Is Your Life—December 2, 1959—NBC

Hosted by Ralph Edwards. Bobby Darin was the subject of this episode of the half hour weekly series. Guests honoring Bobby included Nina Maffia, Vee Vee Maffia, Vana Maffia, Gary Maffia, Charles Maffia, Murray (the K) Kaufman, Norman Taurog, Dick Lord, Sammy Davis, Dick Behrke, George Burns, and Don Kirshner.

The Big Party—December 3, 1959

Hosted by Douglas Fairbanks, Jr. Bobby's songs are unknown.

This Is Darin—1950—Canadian TV Special

Hosted by Bobby Darin. Guests included Clyde McPhatter and Duanne Eddy. Bobby's songs included Mack The Knife, Guys and Dolls, The Gal That Got Away, My Funny Valentine, Beyond The Sea, Clementine, By Myself, A Country Boy (with Eddy).

The Ed Sullivan Show—January 3, 1960—CBS
Hosted by Ed Sullivan. Bobby's songs included You Make Me Feel So Young (with Francis) and You're The Top (with Francis).

The Ed Sullivan Show—February 28, 1960—CBS
Hosted by Ed Sullivan. Bobby's songs are unknown.

The Dick Clark Beechnut Show—March 19, 1960—ABC
Hosted by Dick Clark. Bobby's songs included Beyond The Sea.

The Dick Clark Beechnut Show—June 11, 1960—ABC
Hosted by Dick Clark. Bobby's songs included I'll Be There and Bill Bailey.

Coke Time—June 27, 1960—NBC
Hosted by Pat Boone. Bobby's songs are unknown.

Dan Raven—September 23, 1960—NBC
Drama series starring Skip Homeier. Bobby Darin appeared as himself. His songs included Was there A Call For Me and Bill Bailey. The name of this episode was "The High Cost of Fame."

The Bob Hope Buick Show—October 3, 1960—NBC
Hosted by Bob Hope. Bobby's songs included Artificial Flowers, Lazy River, Two Different Worlds (with Patti Page), Medley: Thanks For The Memory/Mack The Knife/Two Sleepy People (with Hope).

Bobby Darin and Friends—January 31, 1961—NBC
Hosted by Bobby Darin with guest appearances by Joannie Summers and Bob Hope. Bobby's songs included Medley: I Got Rhythm/I Got Plenty of Nothin, I Have Dreamed, Some People, Lucky Pierre (with Hope), I've Had It, I Wish I Were in Love Again (with Summers), Bill Bailey (with Summers and Hope).

The Jackie Gleason Show—March 17, 1961—CBS
Hosted by Jackie Gleason. Bobby's songs included Lazy River, When Irish Eyes Are Smiling. Also included: an excerpt from Darin's March 10, 1956 appearance on *Stage Show*—Bobby singing Rock Island Line.

At This Very Moment—April 1, 1962—ABC
Bobby's songs included Bill Bailey (with Jimmy Durante).

The Ed Sullivan Show—May 6, 1962—CBS
Hosted by Ed Sullivan. Bobby's songs are unknown.

The Merv Griffin Show—October 4, 1962—CBS

Hosted by Merv Griffin. Bobby's songs are unknown.

The Bob Hope Show—November 29, 1962—NBC

Bobby's songs included All Of Me.

Password—January 6, 1963—CBS

Game show hosted by Allen Ludden. Bobby Darin as a celebrity contestant.

The Jerry Lewis Show—Fall, 1963—ABC

Hosted by Jerry Lewis. Bobby's songs included Hello Young Lovers, Some Of These Days, and an impersonation routine incorporating the song One For My Baby.

The Judy Garland Show—December 29, 1963—CBS

Hosted by Judy Garland. Bobbys songs included Swing, Swing, Swing (with Garland and Bob Newhart), Michael Row The Boat Ashore, I'm On My Way, Medley: Sentimental Journey (with Garland), Blues In The Night, Goin' Home (with Garland), Chattanooga Choo Choo, Some Of These Days, Toot Toot Tootsie, I Know That You Know, I've Been Working On the Railroad (with Garland), and Lonesome Road (with Garland).

The Jack Benny Show—January 28, 196—CBS

Hosted by Jack Benny. Bobby's songs included As Long As I'm Singing.

What's My Line—circa 1964—CBS

During the early to mid-1960s, Bobby Darin appeared as a guest on *What's My Line* on several occasions (as part of the panel). No specific dates, however, have been identified.

The Edie Adams Show—February 6, 1964—ABC

Hosted by Edie Adams. Bobby's songs included This Nearly Was Mine, and a Kurt Weill Medley including Mack The Knife, Moon Faced And Starry Eyed, Surghaya Johnny, Here I'll Stay, Bilbao Song, Alabama Song (with Edie Adams).

I've Got A Secret—February 17, 1964—CBS

Hosted by Gary Moore. Bobby Darin appeared as a celebrity contestant. (Darin made several appearances on *I've Got A Secret*. This is the only one for which a specific date has been identified).

Wagon Train—October 4, 1964—ABC

Drama series. Bobby Darin's character was named John Gillman. The episode was entitled "The John Gillman Story."

Bob Hope Chrysler Theater—October 9, 1964—NBC

Drama series. Bobby Darin's character was named Brad Kuber. This episode was entitled "Murder In The First."

The Andy Williams Show—January 11, 1965—NBC

Hosted by Andy Williams. Bobby's songs included Once In A Lifetime, To Be A Performer Medley (with Andy Williams and Vic Damone).

The Match Game—February 1-5, 1965

Hosted by Gene Rayborn. Bobby Darin appeared as a celebrity contestant.

The Andy Williams Show—September, 1965—NBC

Hosted by Andy Williams. Bobby's songs included That Funny Feeling.

The Red Skelton Show—September 21, 1965—CBS

Hosted by Red Skelton. Bobby's songs are unknown.

The Steve Lawrence Show—October 11, 1965—CBS

Hosted by Steve Lawrence. Bobby's songs are unknown.

Something Special—1966—United Kingdom Television Special

A one-man concert starring Bobby Darin. Bobby's songs included Don't Rain On My Parade, About a Quarter To Nine, Once Upon a Time, I Wish I Were In Love Again, Mack The Knife, If I Were A Carpenter, impersonation routine done to One For My Baby, The Girl That Stood Beside Me, Funny What Love Can Do, What'd I Say?, That's All.

The Andy Williams Show—January 10, 1966—NBC

Hosted by Andy Williams. Bobby's songs are unknown.

The Andy Williams Show—circa 1966—NBC

Hosted by Andy Williams. Bobby's songs included Hello Bluebird (with Robert Goulet and Andy Williams), As Long As I'm Singing, I Could Go on Singing (with Robert Goulet and Andy Williams).

Run For Your Life—March 7, 1966—NBC

Drama series starring Ben Gazzara. This was a pilot for a new series which would have starred Bobby Darin. Eve Arden was a guest on this episode which was entitled "Who's Watching the Flespot?" Bobby's character was called Mark Shepherd.

And Debbie Makes Six—January 19, 1967—ABC

Hosted by Debbie Reybnolds. Bobby's songs included Sylvia's Mother (duet with Debbie Reynolds).

Rodgers and Hart Today (aka The Kraft Music Hall)—March 2, 1967—NBC

Hosted by Bobby Darin with guest stars including Diana Ross and The Supremes, Count Basie and His Orchestra, and Petula Clark. Bobby's songs included The Lady Is A Tramp, I Wish I Were In Love Again (with Count Basie and His Orchestra), Any Old Place (with Petula Clark), Falling in Love With Love (with Diana Ross and the Supremes), Mountain Greenery (with Diana Ross and the Supremes, Petula Clark and Count Basie and His Orchestra).

Give My Regards to Broadway (aka The Kraft Music Hall)—October 4, 1967—NBC

Hosted by Bobby Darin with guest star Liza Minnelli. Bobby's songs included Yankee Doodle Dandy and Always Leave 'Em Laughing.

A Grand Night for Singing (aka The Kraft Music Hall)—January 10, 1968—NBC

Hosted by Bobby Darin with guest stars Bobbie Gentry and Bobby Van. Bobby's songs included: Talk to the Animals, Mack the Knife, Drowning in My Tears, Long Time Movin' (with Bobbie Gentry), Nothin' Can Stop Us Now (with Bobbie Gentry and Bobby Van).

The Danny Thomas Show—January 15, 1968—NBC

Drama series. This episode was entitled "The Cage."

Rowan and Martin's Laugh In—October 14, 1968—NBC

Hosted by Dan Rowan and Dick Martin. Bobby's songs included a Mack the Knife parody (with Arte Johnson).

The Andy Williams Show—circa 1969—NBC

Hosted by Andy Williams. Bobby sang Mack the Knife.

Title Unknown (a/k/a The Kraft Music Hall)—January 22, 1969—NBC

Hosted by Bobby Darin with guest stars Stevie Wonder and Judy Collins. Bobby's songs included If I Were a Carpenter (with Stevie Wonder), Help Me Make It Through the Night (with Judy Collins), Splish Splash, and Long Line Rider.

This is Tom Jones—October 2, 1969—ABC

Hosted by Tom Jones. Bobby's songs included Distractions, and a medley of Aquarius and Let the Sunshine In.

The Englebert Humperdinck Show—1970—ABC

Hosted by Englebert Humperdinck with guest star Nancy Wilson. Bobby's songs included Mack the Knife, If I Were a Carpenter, and Blowin' in the Wind (with Nancy Wilson and Englebert Humperdinck.

The Mike Douglas Show—July 21-31, 1970—Syndicated

Hosted by Mike Douglas and Bobby Darin. Bobby's songs included My Funny Valentine.

The Flip Wilson Show—September 24, 1970—NBC

Hosted by Flip Wilson with guest star Roy Clark. Bobby's songs included Melodie and Who Takes Care of the Caretaker's Daughter (with Flip Wilson and Roy Clark).

The Flip Wilson Show—November 20, 1970—NBC

Hosted by Flip Wilson with guest star Sid Caesar. Bobby's songs included Gabriel, a medley including Paddlin' Madelin' Home, Row Row Row (with Flip Wilson), and Noises in the Street (with Flip Wilson and Sid Caesar).

The Flip Wilson Show—January 21, 1971—NBC

Hosted by Flip Wilson. Bobby's songs included Lazy River, If I Were a Carptenter, and Toot Toot Tootsie (with Flip Wilson).

The Darin Invasion—October, 1971—Syndicated

Hosted by Bobby Darin with guests George Burns, Pat Carroll, Linda Ronstadt and The Poppy Family. Bobby's songs included Higher and Higher, Hi-De-Ho, If I Were a Carpenter, and Simple Song of Freedom.

Ironside—October 5, 1971—NBC

Drama series starring Raymond Burr and Don Galloway. This episode was entitled "The Gambling Game."

Cades County—November 28, 1971—CBS

Drama series starring Glenn Ford. This episode was entitled "A Gun For Billy." Bobby's character was called Billy Dobbs.

The Flip Wilson Show—January 13, 1972—NBC

Hosted by Flip Wilson. Bobby's songs included Mack the Knife, Simple Song of Freedom, One of Those Songs (with Flip Wilson).

Night Gallery—February 9, 1972—NBC

Drama series. This episode was entitled "Dead Weight."

The David Frost Show—March, 1972—Syndicated

This was an afternoon talk/variety show hosted by David Frost. Bobby Darin was interviewed by David Frost. His songs included For Once In My Life, Mack the Knife, Splish Splash, If I Were a Carpenter.

The Bobby Darin Amusement Company—July 27, 1972—NBC

Hosted by Bobby Darin with guests George Burns, Burt Reynolds, and Bobbie Gentry. Bobby's songs included Can't Take My Eyes Off Of You, a medley of You Are My Sunshine and Got My Mojo Working, and a medley including Niki Hoeky, Proud Mary, Polk Salad Annie, and Never Ending Song of Love (with Bobbie Gentry).

The Bobby Darin Amusement Company—August 3, 1972—NBC

Hosted by Bobby Darin with guests Debbie Reynolds and Charles Nelson Reilly. Bobby's songs included Charade, Beyond the Sea, and You and Me Babe (with Debbie Reynolds).

The Bobby Darin Amusement Company—August 10, 1972—NBC

Hosted by Bobby Darin with guests Pat Paulsen, Joan Rivers, and Dusty Springfield. Bobby's songs included I'll Be Your Baby Tonight and You've Got a Friend (with Dusty Springfield).

The Bobby Darin Amusement Company—August 17, 1972—NBC

Hosted by Bobby Darin with guests Donald O'Connor, Dionne Warwick, Phil Ford, and Mimi Hines. Bobby's songs included If I Were a Carpenter, Spinning Wheel, Bridge Over Troubled Water (with Dionne Warwick), I'll Never Fall in Love Again (with Donald O'Connor).

The Bobby Darin Amusement Company—August 24, 1972—NBC

Hosted by Bobby Darin with Carl Reiner and Claudine Longet. Bobby's songs included You've Got a Friend (with Claudine Longet).

The Bobby Darin Amusement Company—August 31, 1972—NBC

Hosted by Bobby Darin with Florence Henderson and Pat Paulsen. Bobbys songs included That's All, Artificial Flowers, The Work Song, and Happy Together (with Florence Henderson).

The Bobby Darin Amusement Company—September 7, 1972—NBC

Hosted by Bobby Darin with The Smothers Brothers and Joannie Summers. Bobby's songs included Brother Can You Spare a Dime?, Talk to the Animals, Side by Side (with The Smothers Brothers).

The Sonny and Cher Comedy Hour—November 10, 1972—CBS

Hosted by Sonny Bono and Cher. Bobby's songs included Melodie.

A Matter of Time—December, 1972—NBC

Teenage talk show hosted by Bobby Darin.

The Bobby Darin Show—January 19, 1973—NBC

Hosted by Bobby Darin with guests Burl Ives, Dyan Cannon, and Mimi Hines. Bobby's songs included Once in a Lifetime, Sweet Caroline, About A Quarter to Nine, Happy, Something (with Dyan Cannon).

The Bobby Darin Show—January 26, 1973—NBC

Hosted by Bobby Darin with guests Helen Reddy and David Steinberg. Bobby's songs included Born Free, Caravan, Bridge Over Troubled Water, I'll Be Your Baby Tonight, St. Louis Blues, If Not For You (with Helen Reddy), Meet Me In St. Louis (with Helen Reddy and ensemble).

The Bobby Darin Show—February 2, 1973—NBC

Hosted by Bobby Darin with guests Flip Wilson and Petula Clark. Bobby's songs included Hello Young Lovers, and In the Midnight Hour (with Petula Clark).

The Bobby Darin Show—February 9, 1973—NBC

Hosted by Bobby Darin with guests Redd Foxx, Nancy Sinatra and Seals & Crofts. Bobby's songs included Lover Come Back to Me, King of the Road, Lonesome Road, If, Light My Fire (with Nancy Sinatra), My Kind of Town (with Nancy Sinatra).

The Bobby Darin Show—February 16, 1973—NBC

Hosted by Bobby Darin with guests Joey Heatherton, Charles Nelson Reilly, and Taj Mahal. Bobby's songs included Sixteen Tons.

The Bobby Darin Show—February 23, 1973—NBC

Hosted by Bobby Darin with guests Cloris Leachman and Tim Conway. Bobby's songs included Don't Rain on My Parade, A Nightingale Sang in Barclay Square, Song Sung Blue, Alone Again Naturally, and Never My love (with Cloris Leachman).

The Bobby Darin Show—March 2, 1973—NBC

Hosted by Bobby Darin with guests Elke Sommer, Donald O'Connor, and Charlene Wong. Bobby's songs included It's Today, Mame, Once Upon a Time, Two of a Kind (with Donald O'Connor), Let's Fall in Love (with Elke Sommer), and Give a Little Whistle (with Charlene Wong).

Midnight Special—March 16, 1973—NBC

Hosted by Paul Anka. Bobby's songs included If I Were a Carpenter and a medley including Dream Lover, Bo Diddley, and Splish Splash.

The Bobby Darin Show—March 23, 1973—NBC

Hosted by Bobby Darin with guests Sid Caesar, Dusty Springfield, Jackie Joseph and The Persuasions. Bobby's songs included Some People, Help Me Make It Through the Night, I Get a Kick Out of You, Climb Every Mountain, Baby I Need Your Lovin' (with Dusty Springfield).

The Bobby Darin Show—March 30, 1973—NBC

Hosted by Bobby Darin with guests Andy Griffith, Connie Stevens, Eric Weissberg & Steve Mandel. Bobby's songs included As Long As I'm Singing, Brooklyn Roads, I've Got You Under My Skin, If I Were a Carpenter, and You've Got a Friend (with Connie Stevens).

The Bobby Darin Show—April 6, 1973—NBC

Hosted by Bobby Darin with Phyllis Diller, Leslie Uggums, and David Bromberg. Bobby's songs included Charade, I'll Remember April, Here's That Rainy Day, I'll Be Seeing You, and Happy Together (with Leslie Uggums).

The Bobby Darin Show—April 13, 1973—NBC

Hosted by Bobby Darin with guests Artie Johnson, Freda Payne, and Bread. Bobby's songs included There's A Rainbow Round My Shoulder, Let the Good Times Roll, and Cry Me a River.

The Bobby Darin Show—April 20, 1973—NBC

Hosted by Bobby Darin with guests Carol Lawrence, Pat Buttram, Bill Withers, and Charlene Wong. Bobby's songs included Get Me To The Church on Time, Shilo, Guys and Dolls, Come Rain or Come Shine, Volare, Words (with Carol Lawrence), There's a Hole in the Bucket (with Carol Lawrence), It's De-Lovely (with Carol Lawrence), and High Hopes (with Charlene Wong).

The Bobby Darin Show—April 27, 1973—NBC

Hosted by Bobby Darin with special guest Peggy Lee. Bobby's songs included a medley of For Once In My Life and Once in a Lifetime; Help Me Make it Through the Night; Can't Take My Eyes Off Of You; Bridge Over Troubled Waters,; Midnight Special; Hear that Lonesome Whistle Blow; a medley of You Are My Sunshine, Bo Diddley, and Splish Splash; Just Friends (with Peggy Lee), Something to Remember You By (with Peggy Lee), Skylark (with Peggy Lee), Spring is Here (with Peggy Lee), and Long Ago and Far Away (with Peggy Lee).

This was the last show of Bobby Darin's television series. Although it is unknown on which episode, Bobby Darin also sang the following songs on either The Bobby Darin Amusement Company or The Bobby Darin Show: Draedle, I'll Be Your Baby Tonight, Once Upon a Time, Ain't No Mountain High Enough, St. Louis Woman, Don't Rain on My Parade, Never My Love, You're Nobody Till Somebody Loves You, What Now My Love, Since I Don't Have You, Sail Away, Darling Be Home Soon, Climb Every Mountain, I'm Getting Married in the Morning, All I Have to Do is Dream, Fire and Rain, Let's Fall in Love, and My Kind of Town.

—♪—

Bobby Darin
on Film

PEPE

(Columbia) August 1960

Producer: George Sidney. Director: George Sidney. Film Editors: Viola Lawrence, Al Clark. Set Decorator: William Kiernan. Assistant Director: David Silver. Associate Art Director: Gunther Gerszo. Recording Supervisor: Charles J. Rice. Sound: James Z. Flaster. Choreography: Eugene Loring, Alex Romero. General Music Supervision and Background Score: Johnny Green. Associate Producer: Jacques Gelman. Screenplay: Dorothy Kingsley, Claude Binyon. Screen Story: Leonard Spigelgass, Sonya Levien. Gowns: Edith Head. Art Direction: Ted Haworth. Director of Photography: Joe MacDonald.

CAST: Cantinflas, Dan Dailey, Shirley Jones, Carlos Montalban, Joe Hyams, Maurice Chevalier, Bing Crosby, Michael Callan, Richard Conte, Bobby Darin, Sammy Davis, Jimmy Durante, Zsa Zsa Gabor, Judy Garland, Greer Garson, Hedda Hopper, Joey Bishop, Ernie Kovacs, Peter Lawford, Janet Leigh, Jack Lemmon, Jay North, Kim Novak, Andre Previn, Donna Reed, Debbie Reynolds, Edward G. Robinson, Cesar Romero, Frank Sinatra, Billie Burke, Ann B. Davis, William Demarest, Jack Entratter, Charles Coburn.

COME SEPTEMBER

(Universal) June 1961

Producer: Robert Arthur. Director: Robert Mulligan. Associate Producer: Henry Willson. Screenplay: Stanley Shapiro, Maurice Richlin. Director of Photography: William Daniels. Art Director: Henry Bumstead. Unit Production Supervisor: Ernest Wehmeyer. Unit Production Manager: Sam Gorodisky. Set Director: John Austin. Film Editor: Russell Schoengarth. Sound: Alexander Fisher. Costumes: Morton Haack. Assistant Directors: Joe Kenny, Franco Cirino, John Alarimo. Original Music: Bobby Darin.

CAST: Rock Hudson, Gina Lollabrigida, Sandra Dee, Bobby Darin, Walter Slezak, Brenda de Banzie, Roland Howard, Joel Grey, Michael Eden.

BOBBY'S SONG: Multiplication.

TOO LATE BLUES

(Paramount) January 1962

Producer: John Cassavetes. Director: John Cassavetes. Screenplay: John Cassavetes, Richard Carr. Music: David Raskin. Cinematographer: Lionel Linden. Costumes: Edith Head. Unit

Production Manager: William Mull. Unit Art Director: Tambi Larsen. Assistant Director: Arthur Jacobson. Film Editor: Frank Bracht. Sound: Gene Merritt.

CAST: Bobby Darin, Stella Stevens, Cliff Carnell, Seymour Cassel, Bill Stafford, Richard Chambers, Nick Dennis, Rupert Crosse, Everett Chambers, Vince Edwards, J. Allen Hopkins, Val Avery, James Joyce, Marilyn Clark, Allyson Ames, June Wilkinson.

STATE FAIR

(Twentieth Century Fox) March 1962

Producer: Charles Brackett. Director: Jose Ferrer. Screenplay: Richard Breen. Adaptation: Oscar Hammerstein II, Sonya Levein, Paul Green. Novel: Philip Stang. Music: Richard Rodgers. Lyrics: Oscar Hammerstein II. Additional Songs: Richard Rodgers. Music Supervised and Conducted by: Alfred Newman. Musical Associate: Ken Darby. Choreography: Nick Castle. Director of Photography: William C. Mellor. Art Direction: Jack Martin Smith, Walter Simonds. Assistant Director: Al Schaumer. Costumes: Marjorie Best. Film Editor: David Bretherton. Special Photographic Effects: L. B. Abbott, Emil Kosa, Jr. Sound: Alfred Brunzlin, Warren Delaplain. Orchestrations: George Bassman, Henry Beau, Bennett Carter, Pete King, Gus Levene, Bernard Mayers.

CAST: Pat Boone, Bobby Darin, Pamela Tiffin, Ann-Margaret, Tom Ewell, Alice Faye, Wally Cox, David Brandon, Clem Harvey, Robert Foulk, Linda Henrich, Edward Canutt, Margaret Deramee, Albert Harris, Bebe Allan, George Russell, Edwin McLure, Walter Beilberg.

BOBBY'S SONGS: It's a Grand Night for Singing, This Isn't Heaven.

HELL IS FOR HEROES

(Paramount) June 1962

Producer: Henry Blanke. Director: Don Siegel. Story: Robert Pirosh. Screenplay: Robert Pirosh, Richard Carr. Music: Leonard Rosenman. Sound Recording: Philip Mitchell, John Wilkinson. Art Direction: Hal Pereira, Howard Richmond. Special Photographic Effects: John P. Fulton. Editor: Howard Smith. Assistant Directors: William McGary, James Rosenberger. Technical Advisor: Major William Harrigan, Jr.

CAST: Steve McQueen, Bobby Darin, Fess Parker, Harry Guardino, James Coburn, Mike Kellin, Joseph Hoover, Bill Mullikin, L.Q. Jones, Michele Montau, Don Haggarty, Nick Adams, Bob Newhart.

PRESSURE POINT

(United Artists) September 1962

Producer: Stanley Kramer. Director: Hubert Cornfield. Screenplay: Hubert Cornfield, S. Lee Pogostin. Story: Robert Lindner. Assistant Director: Douglas Green. Cinematography: Ernest

Holler. Music: Ernest Gold. Production Designer: Rudy Sternad. Film Editor: Fred Knudtson. Sound: James Speak. Production Manager: Clem Beauchamp.

CAST: Sidney Poitier, Bobby Darin, Peter Falk, Carl Benton Reid, Mary Munday, Barry Gordon, Howard Caine, Anne Barton, James Anderson, Yvette Vickers, Clegg Hoyt, Richard Bakalayan, Butch Patrick, Lynn Loring.

THE LAST WESTERNER
(Columbia) 1962

Throughout 1962, industry press reported that Bobby Darin was starring in a film entitled *The Last Westerner* for Columbia Pictures. The film was to be produced by Don Diegel and Steve Blauner and was to costar James Cagney and Duane Eddy. The screenplay was based on the Turnley Walker novel, *The Day After the Fourth,* with a script written by Turnley Walker, Don Siegel, and Jack Elam. Although the film is rumored to have been completed, it was not released. No further information about the film is available at this time. Two stills of Bobby Darin in the film do exist.

IF A MAN ANSWERS
(Universal) November 1962

Producer: Ross Hunter. Director: Henry Levin. Screenplay: Richard Morris. Novel: Winifred Wolfe. Photography: Russell Metty. Art Director: Alexander Golitzen. Gowns: Jean Louis. Production Manager: Ernest B. Wehmeyer. Sound: Waldon O. Watson, Frank Wilkinson. Music: Hans Salter. Music Supervision: Joseph Gershenson. Film Editor: Milton Carruth. Assistant Director: Phil Bowles.

CAST: Sandra Dee, Bobby Darin, Micheline Presle, John Lund, Cesar Romero, Stefanie Powers, Christopher Knight, Ted Thorpe, Roger Bacon, John Bleifer, Pamela Searle, Warrene Ott, Dani Lynn, Charlene Holt, Gloria Camacho, Edmay Van Dyke, Rosalee Calveri, Gladys Thornton.

BOBBY'S SONG: If a Man Answers

CAPTAIN NEWMAN, M.D.
(Universal) October 1963

Producer: Robert Arthur. Director: David Miller. Screenplay: Richard Breen, Phoebe and Henry Ephron. Novel: Leo Rosten. Photography: Russell Metty. Art Directors: Alexander Golitzen, Alfred Sweeney. Set Decorator: Howard Bristol. Sound: Walden O. Watson, William Russell. Music: Frank Skinner. Music Supervision: Joseph Gershenson. Second Unit Director: Robert D. Webb. Unit Production Manager: Joseph Behm. Technical Advisors: Major B.A. Whitaker, Captain Sherwyn Woods. Film Editor: Alma Macroril. Costumes: Rosemary Odell. Assistant Director: Phil Bowles.

CAST: Gregory Peck, Tony Curtis, Angie Dickinson, Bobby Darin, Eddie Albert, James Gregory, Bethel Leslie, Robert Duvall, Jane Withers, Dick Sargent, Larry Storch, Robert F. Simon, Syl Lamont, Paul Carr, Vito Scotti, Crahan Denton, Gregory Walcott, Charles Briggs.

THAT FUNNY FEELING

Universal) October 1965

Producer: Harry Keller. Director: Richard Thorpe. Photography: Clifford Stine. Production Manager: Howard Pine. Art Director: George Webb. Film Editor: Gene Milford. Sound: Waldon O. Watson, Lyle Cain. Assistant Directors: Joe Kenny, James Welch.

CAST: Sandra Dee, Bobby Darin, Donald O'Connor, Nita Talbot, Larry Storch, James Westerfield, Leo G. Carrol, Gregory Shannon, Robert Straus, Ben Lessy, Frank Killmond.

BOBBY'S SONG: That Funny Feeling.

GUNFIGHT IN ABILENE

(Universal) July 1966

Producer: Howard Christie. Director: William Hole. Screenplay: John D.F. Black. Director of Photography: Maury Gertsman. Unit Production Manager: Bill Gilmore. Assistant Directors: Joe Kenny, James Welch, Ron Grow. Unit Publicist: Walter Burrell. Cameraman: Maury Gertsman. Art Director: Bill DeCinces. Film Editor: Cliff Bell, Jr. Script Supervisor: Bob Forrest. Sound Technicians: Frank Wilkinson, Bill Griffith, Jack Danskin. Wardrobe: Hugh McFarland, Larry Harmell, Francis Hamilton. Special Effects: Roland Skeet. Original Music: Bobby Darin.

CAST: Bobby Darin, Emily Banks, Leslie Nielson, Don Galloway, Donnelly Rhodes, Frank McGrath, Barbara Werle, Michael Sarrazen, William Phipps, Bill Mims, Johnny Seven, Don Dubbins, Robert Sorrells, Myron Healey, James McCallion, Bryan O'Byrne.

BOBBY'S SONG: Amy.

COP OUT

(Rank) February 1968

(Released in Great Britain in 1967 under the title Stranger in the House.*)*

Producer: Dimitri de Greenwald. Director: Pierre Rouve. Screenplay: Pierre Rouve. Novel: Georges Simenon. Photography: Ken Higgins. Music: Patrick John Scott. Art Director: Tony Woollard. Editor: Ernest Wabler.

CAST: James Mason, Geraldine Chaplin, Bobby Darin, Paul Bertoya, Ian Ogilvy, Bryan Stanyon, Pippa Steel, Clive Morton, James Hayter, Megs Jenkins, Lisa Donnelly, Moira Lester, yootha Joyce, John Menderson, Rita Webb, Danners Walker, Julian Orchard, Ivar Dean, Marjorie Lawrence, Lindy Aaron, Lucy Griffiths.

THE HAPPY ENDING

(United Artists) December 1969

Producer: Richard Brooks. Director: Richard Brooks. Screenplay: Richard Brooks. Photography: Conrad Hall. Music: Michel Legrand. Lyrics: Marilyn and Alan Bergman. Film Editor: George Greenville. Sound: William Randall, Jr. Special Effects: Chuck Gaspar. Assistant Director: Tom Shaw.

CAST: Jean Simmons, John Forsythe, Lloyd Bridges, Teresa Wright, Dick Shawn, Nanette Fabray, Bobby Darin, Tina Louise, Kathy Fields, Karen Steele.

THE VENDORS

From 1969 to 1973, Bobby Darin was involved in the production of a film entitled *The Vendors*. The film was produced, directed, and musically scored by Bobby Darin, with a screenplay written by Bobby Darin. Although the film was completed, a cast and credit list is unavailable. The leading roles in the film were played by Mariette Hartley, Dick Lord, Gary Wood, and Richard Bakalayan. At the time of his death, Bobby was still looking for a distributor. The film is now in the hands of the Darin estate.

HAPPY MOTHERS DAY . . . LOVE, GEORGE

(Taurean/Cinema 5) August 1973

(Released to television as *Run, Stranger, Run*)

Producer: Darren McGavin. Director: Darren McGavin. Screenplay: Robert Clouse. Photography: Walter Lassally. Music: Don Vincent. Editor: George Grenville. Sound: Hal Lewis, Richard Portman, Evelyn Rutledge. Costumes: Robert Anton, Anne Klein, Pierre Cardin. Production Supervisor: Leon Chooluck. Production Coordinator: Maria-Luisa Alcaraz. Assistant Director: Scott Maitland.

CAST: Patricia Neal, Cloris Leachman, Bobby Darin, Tessa Dahl, Ron Howard, Kathie Browne, Joe Mascolo, Simon Oakland, Thayer David, Gale Garnett, Roy Applegate, Jan Chamberlain, Gerald E. Forbes, Orest Ulan, Clarence Greene Jeans.

—♪—

The Unreleased Recordings of Bobby Darin

Throughout Bobby Darin's recording career (1957–1973) he recorded dozens of songs, which were never released. In some cases, there is every reason to believe that they may ultimately be packaged by Atlantic, Capitol, or Motown in compact disc form. Others have been lost forever. Following details those that have been identified:

October 29, 1958 (ATCO)
Some of These Days (early version); Didn't It Feel Good? These were not recorded with a specific album in mind.

May 19-21, 1959 (ATCO)
The Breeze and I; Since My Love Was Gone; The Lamp Is Low. These were recorded for the album *This Is Darin*.

February 1-2, 1960 (ATCO)
A Game of Poker; I Got a Woman. These were recorded for the album *Winners*.

June 15-16, 1960 (ATCO)
Birth of the Blues; My Funny Valentine; Splish Splash. These were live recordings made at the Copa in New York City. They were deleted from the album *Darin at the Copa* before its release.

August 14, 17 and 22, 1960 (ATCO)
Back in Your Own Backyard; Lily of Laguna; Cecelia. These were recorded with Johnny Mercer for the album *Bobby Darin and Johnny Mercer: Two of a Kind*.

March 25, 1961 (ATCO)
Bobby's Blues. This recording was not made with any specific album in mind.

June 6, 1961 (ATCO)
Special Someone; Teenage Theme; Movin' On. These recordings were from the soundtrack of the film *Come September*.

August 19, 1965 (Atlantic)

Sweet Memories of You; Ain't That a Bunch of Nonsense. These recordings were made to be released as 45-rpm singles.

August 23, 1965 (Atlantic)

Baby I Miss You. This recording was not made with a particular album in mind.

December 13-15, 1965; March 23, 1966 (Atlantic)

Ace in the Hole; The Best is Yet to Come; The Sheik of Araby; This Could Be the Start of Something Big; I Got Plenty of Nothing; Baby Won't You Please Come Home; Strangers in the Night. These recordings were recorded for inclusion in the album *The Shadow of Your Smile*.

February 4, 1966 (Atlantic)

Weeping Willow. This recording was planned as the "B" side of a 45-rpm release of the Darin song Rainin'.

April 21, 1966 (Atlantic)

True Love Are Blessing. This recording was not made with a particular album in mind.

June 21, 1966 (Atlantic)

Merry Go Round in the Rain. This recording was not made with a particular album in mind.

August 1, 1966 (Atlantic)

L. A. Breakdown; I Can Live on Love; Manhattan in My Heart; Lulu's Back in Town; Mountain Greenery; For You; What Now My Love; It's Magic; Danke Schoen; My Own True Love; On a Clear Day You Can See Forever; A Quarter to Nine; Seventeen. These recordings were made for an album, which was never released. The master tapes were lost in a fire at Atlantic's headquarters.

November 1, 1966 (Atlantic)

Funny What Love Can Do (alternate version;) Good Day Sunshine; Younger Girl. These recordings were deleted from the album *If I Were a Carpenter*.

March 28, 1967 (Direction)

Saginaw, Michigan. This recording was not made with a particular album in mind.

November 13, 18, and 19, 1967 (Direction)

My Baby Needs Me; All Strung Out; Tupelo Mississippi Flash; Natural Soul Loving Big City Countrified Man; When I'm Gone. These recordings were not made with a particular album in mind.

1969 (Label Unconfirmed)

Bobby Darin's nightclub act at The Bonanza was recorded for release as a live album. The album was never released, and the actual contents are unconfirmed. One song from this album (I'll Be Your Baby Tonight) was eventually released on a Rhino boxed set, so the recordings do still exist.

Additionally, Motown's records show that during Bobby's brief tenure at the label, the following recordings were made—none of them have been released, and specific dates of the recording sessions are unavailable: Higher and Higher, I Don't Know How to Love Her; Catch the Wind; Time Will Tell; Soft Spoken woman; Smilin' Through; Help Me Mama; Lady Madonna; You've Lost That Loving Feeling; I Walk the Line; Watch the River Flow; Tango; I'm Glad About It; Oh Lord Where's My Baby; Child of Tears.

♪

Index